AW 180 Companion
for the Daily Promises of God for Educators

Where we read the Bible with our brother and sisters in the public schools

New International Version

THE HOLY BIBLE, NEW INTERNATIONAL VERSION®, NIV® Copyright © 1973, 1978, 1984, 2011 by Biblica, Inc.® Used by permission. All rights reserved worldwide.

Living Bible

The Living Bible copyright © 1971 by Tyndale House Foundation. Used by permission of Tyndale House Publishers Inc., Carol Stream, Illinois 60188. All rights reserved. The Living Bible, TLB, and the The Living Bible logo are registered trademarks of Tyndale House Publishers.

Revised Standard Version (RSV)

Revised Standard Version of the Bible, copyright © 1946, 1952, and 1971 the Division of Christian Education of the National Council of the Churches of Christ in the United States of America. Used by permission. All rights reserved.

King James
The KJV is public domain in the United States.

ISBN 13:978-15448995727

 Where we read the Bible with our brother and sisters in the public schools

NOTE TO THE EDUCATOR

Dear Christian educator,

This Around the Word in 180 Days Companion is the basic transcript of our daily podcast. Each school day we read the Bible with our brothers and sisters in the public schools. In the 2014-2015 school year, we read the New Testament together. In the 2015-2016, we read all the Psalms and Proverbs. This year we are reading the promises of God in four translations. Whether you join us on Around the Word in 180 Days podcast or not, I encourage you to be in the Word and prayer daily. The benefit of AW 180 is that you can easily play it while you are driving to or from school. It's in our CEAI app, in iTunes and on the web and can be played at your convenience. Use the QR code on the last page for a direct link. My goal is to encourage, equip and empower you in your high calling through Biblical principles.

During a sermon by Dr. Barry Black, our US Senate chaplain, we were admonished to study the promises of God. While gathering the promises I noticed that I had nearly 180! It was then that I felt convicted to share them with Christian educators on our program. There are a few books out there with the Promises of God for educators and all of them present the promises by categories: love, peace, patience, encouragement and more. I felt led to categorize them as they appeared in the Bible. From Genesis to Revelation, God has been a Promise Keeper. I understand that it is not theologically correct to pull a verse out of context. These promises are meant to be encouragement for you, the educator in the public schools. As I read each one in four translations, I wrote a small note of encouragement with the understanding that God will speak to you through His Word in His own way. May you be richly blessed through the study of His promises this school year.

I will be releasing one promise a day with the AW 180 program each school day and will also be providing the verse against a sunrise background that I have taken to share the beauty of His creation. (see a sample on the next page)

With all my love to you. May you bless your students this year as your represent Jesus Christ as His ambassador.

Prayerfully yours,

Karen C. Seddon
kseddon@ceai.org
www.aw180days.com

DAILY PROMISES OF GOD
for educators

©2016 Christian Educators Association International. All rights reserved.

#iamachristianeducator

 Where we read the Bible with our brother and sisters in the public schools

SAMPLE PROMISE CARDS

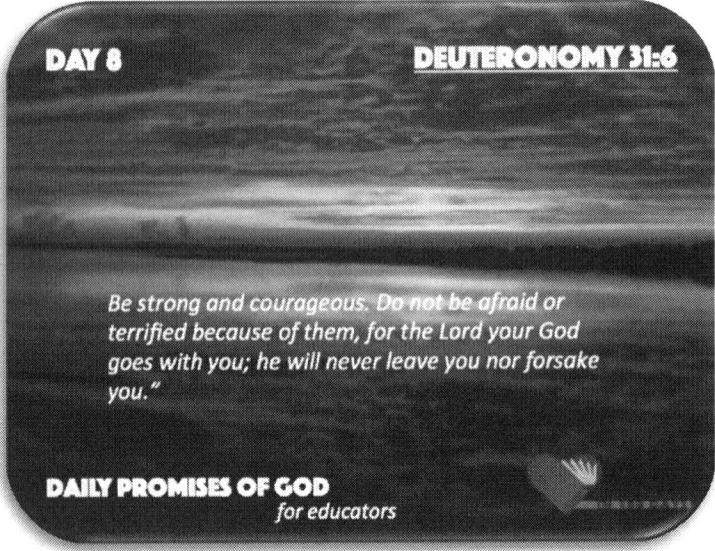

DAILY PROMISES OF GOD
for educators

©2016 Christian Educators Association International. All rights reserved.

#iamachristianeducator

 Where we read the Bible with our brother and sisters in the public schools

AN ABC PRAYER OF ADORATION

Each Around the World in 180 Days show opens with an ABC Prayer of Adoration. These are just a few of the names and adjectives used to give Him praise.

A – Advocate, Author of our Faith, Alpha and Omega, All and All, the Amen, Anchor, Ancient of Days, Attentive, the Answer, Awesome, Avenger, Active on our behalf, Abba

B – Beloved, Branch, Bishop of our souls, Beyond description, Bridegroom, Only Begotten Son, Bright Morning Star, Beautiful, Blessed, Builder, Bountiful, Beginning and End, Boss

C – Christ Alone, Carpenter, Chief Cornerstone, Covenant Keeping God, Counselor, Comforter, Caring, Close to us, Our Confidence, Consoling, Creator of all things, Cleanser

D – Door, Deliverer, Divine Redeemer, Desire of our hearts, Dominion, Defender, Dayspring

E – Eternal, Everlasting Father, Encouraging, Enthroned, Ever Loving, Enduring, Elohim, El Elyon (God Most High), Exalted One, God of Everywhere, Enduringly Strong, Exalted

F – Father, Faithful, Fearless, Finisher of our faith, Forgiving, Fulfilling Forever and ever, Fountain of Life, Forerunner, Faithfulness, Final Authority, Fullness of Grace

G – God, Gracious, Good, Gorgeous, Good Shepard, the Great I AM, Guide, Guardian, Gift, Give, the Great God of Creation, Glory, God of the generations, Gentle Shepherd

H – Healer, Holy, Head of the Church, Hope of Israel, Heir of all things, Helper, Happy, High Priest, Hope, Help in ages past, High Standards, Holy Spirit, Helmet of Salvation

I – Immanuel, Intercessor, Incredible, Intelligent Designer, Image of the Invisible God, I AM, Instructor, God of Increase, God of the Impossible, Incomparable, Inheritance, Immortal

J – Jesus, Judge, Justification, Jealous, Joy, Just in time God, Jehovah Jirah (Provider), Jehovah Nissi (Banner), Jehovah Rohi (Shepherd), Jevovah Tsaba (Warrior)

K – King of Kings, Keeper of our souls, Kinsmen Redeemer, Key to everything, King of Israel, Kind

L – Lord of Lords, Love, Leader, Liberty, Living Water, Light of the World, Loving God, Lamb of God, Light unto our paths, Lamp unto our feet, Living God, Limitless, Lord Forevermore

M – Mighty, Merciful, Messiah, Man of Sorrows, Mindful, Manifesting, Mediator, Maker of all things, Mender of the Broken, Most High God

DAILY PROMISES OF GOD
for educators

 Where we read the Bible with our brother and sisters in the public schools

AN ABC PRAYER OF ADORATION

N – New today, Name above all names, Near to us, Never failing, New mercies each day, Nothing is Impossible, Nurturing, Noble, Never changing

O – Omnipotent, Omnipresent, Omniscient, Only wise God, Only Begotten Son, Opener of our eyes, Opener of our hearts, Overcomer, Offering, Over all, Omega, Owner, One true living God

P – Prince of Peace, Prophet, Protector, Passionate One, Preserving God, Promisor, Powerful, Perfecter of our faith, Purchaser of our blood, Provider, Priceless, God of Possibilities, Planner, Purity, Perseverance

Q – Quieter of our souls, Quickener, Quick to hear us, Quintessential essence of all that has ever been and will ever be

R – Resurrection and the Life, Rock, Redeemer, Refuge, Reigning God, Ruler, Renowned, Reconciler, Rich, Righteousness, Rider on the White Horse, Robed in Majesty

S – Son of God, Son of Man, Salvation, Stability of our times, Savior, Good Shepherd, Servant, Sure Foundation, Sinless, Slow to anger, Sun and Shield, Spirit, Supreme

T – Testimony, Trusted One, Teacher of Teachers, the One we want to touch, Truth, True Witness, Trustworthy, Triumphant, True Vine

U – Unmatched, Unbelievable, Ubiquitously Ours, Understanding, Underwriter of all things, Upright, Unchanging, Upholder of our lives

V – Vindicator, Very good, Visionary, Voice, Victory, Vinedresser, Victorious Warrior

W – Word, Wonderful, Wisdom, Worthy, Wonderful Counselor, Watchful, the Way and the Life and the Truth, Witness, Was and is and is to come, Warrior

X – eXpert, eXcellent, eXtraordinary, eXtra special, eXample

Y – Yashua, Yahweh, Yesterday, today and tomorrow, the One we want to say Yes to, the One we want to Yield to, His Yoke is easy

Z – Zenith, Zealous, God of Zion, Zero tolerance for sin

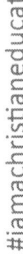

DAILY PROMISES OF GOD
for educators

Where we read the Bible with our brother and sisters in the public schools

DAILY PROMISES OF GOD
for educators

GENESIS 8:21-22

NIV - *The Lord smelled the pleasing aroma and said in his heart: "Never again will I curse the ground because of humans, even though every inclination of the human heart is evil from childhood. And never again will I destroy all living creatures, as I have done. "As long as the earth endures, seedtime and harvest, cold and heat, summer and winter, day and night will never cease."*

RSV - *And when the Lord smelled the pleasing odor, the Lord said in his heart, "I will never again curse the ground because of man, for the imagination of man's heart is evil from his youth; neither will I ever again destroy every living creature as I have done. While the earth remains, seedtime and harvest, cold and heat, summer and winter, day and night, shall not cease."*

KJV - *And the Lord smelled a sweet savour; and the Lord said in his heart, I will not again curse the ground any more for man's sake; for the imagination of man's heart is evil from his youth; neither will I again smite any more every thing living, as I have done. While the earth remaineth, seedtime and harvest, and cold and heat, and summer and winter, and day and night shall not cease.*

LB - *And Jehovah was pleased with the sacrifice and said to himself, "I will never do it again— I will never again curse the earth, destroying all living things, even though man's bent is always toward evil from his earliest youth, and even though he does such wicked things. As long as the earth remains, there will be springtime and harvest, cold and heat, winter and summer, day and night."*

NOTE TO THE EDUCATOR

Don't let your heart be troubled over the small things. Our God is above all things. He has promised that day and night will never cease until He ushers in His kingdom. Let today's worries be shadowed by His great promise of eternity which is much bigger than our school life!

1:16 PM PRAYER

Please pray that we will do all things for the glory of God.

QUOTE FOR THE DAY

The beautiful thing about learning is that no one can take it away from you. **B.B. King**

NOTES:

___

___

___

___

___

Where we read the Bible with our brother and sisters in the public schools

DAILY PROMISES OF GOD
for educators

EXODUS 15:26

NIV - *If you listen carefully to the Lord your God and do what is right in his eyes, if you pay attention to his commands and keep all his decrees, I will not bring on you any of the diseases I brought on the Egyptians, for I am the Lord, who heals you.*

RSV – *If you will diligently hearken to the voice of the Lord your God, and do that which is right in his eyes, and give heed to his commandments and keep all his statutes, I will put none of the diseases upon you which I put upon the Egyptians; for I am the Lord, your healer.*

KJV – *If thou wilt diligently hearken to the voice of the Lord thy God, and wilt do that which is right in his sight, and wilt give ear to his commandments, and keep all his statutes, I will put none of these diseases upon thee, which I have brought upon the Egyptians: for I am the Lord that healeth thee.*

LB - *If you will listen to the voice of the Lord your God, and obey it, and do what is right, then I will not make you suffer the diseases I sent on the Egyptians, for I am the Lord who heals you.*

NOTE TO THE EDUCATOR
Doing what is right in His eyes is paramount to our Christian walk. Fostering an environment in our classroom where we always do the right thing is equally important. Our students watch our every move. Let us seek God's presence to always do the right thing before Him and those we interact with each day at school.

1:16 PM PRAYER

Please pray for a peace that surpasses all understanding.

QUOTE FOR THE DAY
Children have never been very good at listening to their elders, but they have never failed to imitate them. **James Baldwin**

NOTES:
_____
_____
_____
_____
_____

Where we read the Bible with our brother and sisters in the public schools

DAILY PROMISES OF GOD
for educators

NUMBERS 6:24-26

NIV - *The Lord bless you and keep you;*
the Lord make his face shine on you and be gracious to you;
the Lord turn his face toward you and give you peace.

RSV - *The Lord bless you and keep you:*
The Lord make his face to shine upon you, and be gracious to you:
The Lord lift up his countenance upon you, and give you peace.

KJV - *The Lord bless thee, and keep thee:*
The Lord make his face shine upon thee, and be gracious unto thee:
The Lord lift up his countenance upon thee, and give thee peace.

LB - *May the Lord bless and protect you;*
may the Lord's face radiate with joy because of you;
may he be gracious to you, show you his favor, and give you his peace.

NOTE TO THE EDUCATOR

Accept this gracious promise of the Lord for you today, but take this challenge. Before the day begins and you have any student or colleague contact, say **Numbers 6:24-26** over their life. Commit it to memory so that you can bless them each and every school day.

1:16 PM PRAYER

Please pray for the needs of the technology leader on your campus.

QUOTE FOR THE DAY

The difference between school and life? In school, you're taught a lesson and then given a test. In life you are given a test that teaches you a lesson. **Tom Bodett**

NOTES:

_____
_____
_____
_____
_____

DAY 3

#iamachristianeducator

Where we read the Bible with our brother and sisters in the public schools

DAILY PROMISES OF GOD
for educators

DEUTERONOMY 4:7

DAY 4

NIV - *What other nation is so great as to have their gods near them the way the Lord our God is near us whenever we pray to him?*

RSV - *For what great nation is there that has a god so near to it as the Lord our God is to us, whenever we call upon him?*

KJV - *For what nation is there so great, who hath God so nigh unto them, as the Lord our God is in all things that we call upon him for?*

LB - *For what other nation, great or small, has God among them, as the Lord our God is here among us whenever we call upon him?*

NOTE TO THE EDUCATOR

When we pray, our God draws near to us. Who else has a God so near than the Christian educator? Pray continually with thanksgiving and seek His presence in your school. Where there are Christian educators, He is there. Find another colleague to pray with and encourage each other to remember just how near He is!

1:16 PM PRAYER

Please pray for the joy of the Lord to be our strength. (Neh. 8:10)

QUOTE FOR THE DAY

Strive not to be a success, but rather to be of value.   **Albert Einstein**

NOTES:

_____
_____
_____
_____
_____

#iamachristianeducator

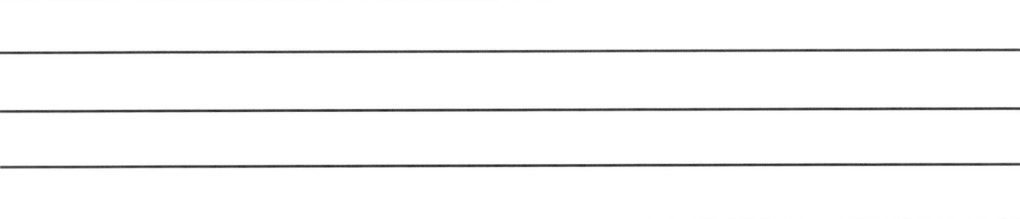

Where we read the Bible with our brother and sisters in the public schools

DAILY PROMISES OF GOD
for educators

DEUTERONOMY 4:31

DAY 5

NIV - *For the Lord your God is a merciful God; he will not abandon or destroy you or forget the covenant with your ancestors, which he confirmed to them by oath.*

RSV - *For the Lord your God is a merciful God; he will not fail you or destroy you or forget the covenant with your fathers which he swore to them.*

KJV - *For the Lord thy God is a merciful God; he will not forsake thee, neither destroy thee, nor forget the covenant of thy fathers which he sware unto them.*

LB - *For the Lord your God is merciful—he will not abandon you nor destroy you nor forget the promises he has made to your ancestors.*

NOTE TO THE EDUCATOR

He will NEVER leave you! He is the God of promises and He cannot lie. I'm sure you would love to tell your students that you will never abandon them nor fail to support them. It will always be the intention of our hearts, but we are human and we can't make such a promise. But God has promised that to us, his children. Take courage, Christian educator, He will never forget His promises.

1:16 PM PRAYER

Please pray for patience with God's plans for us.

QUOTE FOR THE DAY

People often say that motivation doesn't last. Well, neither does bathing. That's why we recommend it daily. **Zig Ziglar**

NOTES:

_____
_____
_____
_____
_____

#iamachristianeducator

Where we read the Bible with our brother and sisters in the public schools

DAILY PROMISES OF GOD
for educators

DEUTERONOMY 7:9

DAY 6

NIV - *Know therefore that the Lord your God is God; he is the faithful God, keeping his covenant of love to a thousand generations of those who love him and keep his commandments.*

RSV - *Know therefore that the Lord your God is God, the faithful God who keeps covenant and steadfast love with those who love him and keep his commandments, to a thousand generations.*

KJV - *Know therefore that the Lord thy God, he is God, the faithful God, which keepeth covenant and mercy with them that love him and keep his commandments to a thousand generations.*

LB - *Understand, therefore, that the Lord your God is the faithful God who for a thousand generations keeps his promises and constantly loves those who love him and who obey his commands.*

NOTE TO THE EDUCATOR

We serve a covenant God Who keeps His promises for a thousand generations! What a mighty God we serve. Our profession is uniquely qualified to touch generations. After being in the profession a while, it is amazing to teach the children of our original students. Don't let that discourage you. Know that you are serving them as the Lord blesses your obedience to the next generation. It is an honor to have the high calling of educator.

1:16 PM PRAYER

Please pray that our classrooms will be places of mercy and grace.

QUOTE FOR THE DAY

It is impossible to rightly govern a nation without God and the Bible. **George Washington**

NOTES:

_____

_____

_____

_____

_____

#iamachristianeducator

Where we read the Bible with our brother and sisters in the public schools

DAILY PROMISES OF GOD
for educators

DEUTERONOMY 28:4

DAY 7

NIV - *The fruit of your womb will be blessed, and the crops of your land and the young of your livestock—the calves of your herds and the lambs of your flocks.*

RSV - *Blessed shall be the fruit of your body, and the fruit of your ground, and the fruit of your beasts, the increase of your cattle, and the young of your flock.*

KJV - *Blessed shall be the fruit of thy body, and the fruit of thy ground, and the fruit of thy cattle, the increase of thy kine, and the flocks of thy sheep.*

LB - *These are the blessings that will come upon you:*
  Blessings in the city,
  Blessings in the field;
  Many children,
  Ample crops,
  Large flocks and herds;
  Blessings of fruit and bread;
  Blessings when you come in,
  Blessings when you go out.

NOTE TO THE EDUCATOR

Praise God from Whom all blessings flow. Praise Him ye creatures here below. Praise Him above ye heavenly hosts. Praise Father, Son and Holy Ghost. Amen. Have you stopped to thank God today for the blessings of being an educator? It's the greatest career in the world because other careers would not exist without educators! Praise God.

1:16 PM PRAYER

Please pray for endurance and good judgment for our NEW teachers.

QUOTE FOR THE DAY

If you can dream it, you can do it. **Walt Disney**

NOTES:
_____
_____
_____
_____
_____

#iamachristianeducator

 *Where we read the Bible with our brother and sisters in the public schools*

DAILY PROMISES OF GOD
for educators

DEUTERONOMY 31:6

DAY 8

NIV - *Be strong and courageous. Do not be afraid or terrified because of them, for the Lord your God goes with you; he will never leave you nor forsake you.*

RSV - *Be strong and of good courage, do not fear or be in dread of them: for it is the Lord your God who goes with you; he will not fail you or forsake you.*

KJV - *Be strong and of a good courage, fear not, nor be afraid of them: for the Lord thy God, he it is that doth go with thee; he will not fail thee, nor forsake thee.*

LB - *Be strong! Be courageous! Do not be afraid of them! For the Lord your God will be with you. He will neither fail you nor forsake you.*

NOTE TO THE EDUCATOR

When we were kids we could never imagine a teacher being afraid, but now that we are the teacher, administrator or paraprofessional, we become afraid from time to time. Be strong and of good courage because we serve a mighty God Who goes before us in our classrooms, hallways and all areas of our school. Find a colleague who can come along side you in agreement with this promise if you ever feel afraid.

1:16 PM PRAYER

Please pray for our colleagues who are having financial difficulties.

QUOTE FOR THE DAY

Do what you can, with what you have, where you are. **Theodore Roosevelt**

NOTES:

_____
_____
_____
_____
_____

#iamachristianeducator

Where we read the Bible with our brother and sisters in the public schools

DAILY PROMISES OF GOD
for educators

DEUTERONOMY 31:8

NIV - *The Lord himself goes before you and will be with you; he will never leave you nor forsake you. Do not be afraid; do not be discouraged.*

RSV - *It is the Lord who goes before you; he will be with you, he will not fail you or forsake you; do not fear or be dismayed.*

KJV - *And the Lord, he it is that doth go before thee; he will be with thee, he will not fail thee, neither forsake thee: fear not, neither be dismayed.*

LB - *Don't be afraid, for the Lord will go before you and will be with you; he will not fail nor forsake you.*

DAY 9

NOTE TO THE EDUCATOR

When you walk on campus this morning, picture the Lord going before you. He is truly with you every step of the day as He is with all Christian educators and Christian students. What an army we truly are, yet somehow we think there are no other Christians around. Ask God to show you those He is leading and guiding so that you can be strengthened in unity.

1:16 PM PRAYER

Please pray that all the technologies work today.

QUOTE FOR THE DAY

Today you are You, that is truer than true. There is no one alive who is Youer than You.
Dr. Suess

NOTES:
_____
_____
_____
_____
_____

#iamachristianeducator

 *Where we read the Bible with our brother and sisters in the public schools*

DAILY PROMISES OF GOD
for educators

JOSHUA 1:9

D A Y   1 0

NIV - *Have I not commanded you? Be strong and courageous. Do not be afraid; do not be discouraged, for the Lord your God will be with you wherever you go.*

RSV - *Have I not commanded you? Be strong and of good courage; be not frightened, neither be dismayed; for the Lord your God is with you wherever you go.*

KJV - *Have not I commanded thee? Be strong and of a good courage; be not afraid, neither be thou dismayed: for the Lord thy God is with thee whithersoever thou goest.*

LB - *Yes, be bold and strong! Banish fear and doubt! For remember, the Lord your God is with you wherever you go.*

NOTE TO THE EDUCATOR

Be holy bold! I had a great mentor for years who told me each and every time to be "Holy Bold." He never once explained what it meant, but I knew that I had the encouragement to be a Christian educator in the public schools. I prayed with boldness, I invited others to join in prayer and I learned what I can and cannot do in the public schools while being bold, yet gracious. What about you? Are you "Holy Bold?"

1:16 PM PRAYER

Please pray for safety and rest for students and staff over this Labor Day weekend.

QUOTE FOR THE DAY

May the God of hope fill you with all joy and peace in believing, so that by the power of the Holy Spirit you may abound in hope. **Romans 15:13**

NOTES:

_____
_____
_____
_____
_____

#iamachristianeducator

Where we read the Bible with our brother and sisters in the public schools

DAILY PROMISES OF GOD
for educators

JOSHUA 23:14

NIV - *Now I am about to go the way of all the earth. You know with all your heart and soul that not one of all the good promises the Lord your God gave you has failed. Every promise has been fulfilled; not one has failed.*

RSV - *And now I am about to go the way of all the earth, and you know in your hearts and souls, all of you, that not one thing has failed of all the good things which the Lord your God promised concerning you; all have come to pass for you, not one of them has failed.*

KJV - *And, behold, this day I am going the way of all the earth: and ye know in all your hearts and in all your souls, that not one thing hath failed of all the good things which the Lord your God spake concerning you; all are come to pass unto you, and not one thing hath failed thereof.*

LB - *Soon I will be going the way of all the earth—I am going to die. You know very well that God's promises to you have all come true.*

NOTE TO THE EDUCATOR

Think of all the prayers and sacrifices it took to become an educator. There was no simple path. Did you pray and ask God for His help? If so, look at how faithful He is to fulfill your dream to become an educator. If you didn't pray for His help, He was faithful to your unspoken desires. He is a great God of promises and fulfillment. Thank Him right now for His unfailing love.

1:16 PM PRAYER

Please pray that our students have wisdom when choosing the music they listen to and the TV shows they watch.

QUOTE FOR THE DAY

Throw kindness around like confetti. - **Unknown**

NOTES:

_____
_____
_____
_____
_____

DAY 11

#iamachristianeducator

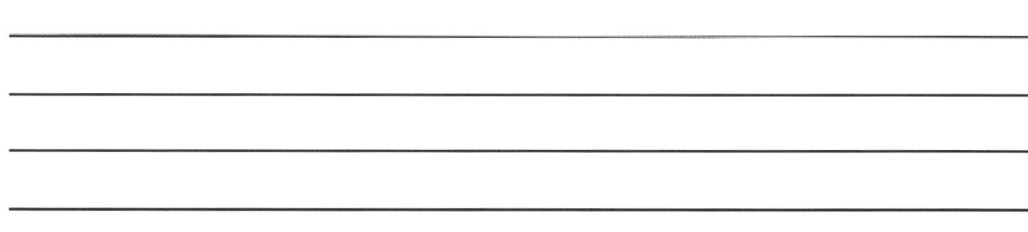
Where we read the Bible with our brother and sisters in the public schools

DAILY PROMISES OF GOD
for educators

1ST SAMUEL 12:22

DAY 12

NIV - *For the sake of his great name the Lord will not reject his people, because the Lord was pleased to make you his own.*

RSV - *For the Lord will not cast away his people, for his great name's sake, because it has pleased the Lord to make you a people for himself.*

KJV - *For the Lord will not forsake his people for his great name's sake: because it hath pleased the Lord to make you his people.*

LB - *The Lord will not abandon his chosen people, for that would dishonor his great name. He made you a special nation for himself—just because he wanted to!*

NOTE TO THE EDUCATOR

The Lord has set us aside as His people that we may worship His holy name. Christian educators in the public schools are brothers and sisters in the same family of God. Oh what a great heavenly family it will be, yet in the meantime we are His chosen people, His ambassadors in our schools. Dear Lord, please help us to be salt and light, love and mercy and all things that bring You honor and glory. Amen.

1:16 PM PRAYER

Please pray to remember that each child is fearfully and wonderfully made (Ps. 139:14)

QUOTE FOR THE DAY

What sculpture is to a block of marble, education is to the human soul. **Joseph Addison**

NOTES:
_____
_____
_____
_____
_____

#iamachristianeducator

Where we read the Bible with our brother and sisters in the public schools

DAILY PROMISES OF GOD
for educators ## 2ND CHRONICLES 7:14

NIV - *If my people, who are called by my name, will humble themselves and pray and seek my face and turn from their wicked ways, then I will hear from heaven, and I will forgive their sin and will heal their land.*

RSV - *If my people who are called by my name humble themselves, and pray and seek my face, and turn from their wicked ways, then I will hear from heaven, and will forgive their sin and heal their land.*

KJV - *If my people, which are called by my name, shall humble themselves, and pray, and seek my face, and turn from their wicked ways; then will I hear from heaven, and will forgive their sin, and will heal their land.*

LB - *Then if my people will humble themselves and pray, and search for me, and turn from their wicked ways, I will hear them from heaven and forgive their sins and heal their land.*

NOTE TO THE EDUCATOR

We need a healing in our land. We need a healing in our schools. It's up to us, brothers and sisters in the public schools, to humble ourselves and pray and to seek His face and turn from our wicked ways. It is His promise that He will hear our cry, forgive us and heal our land. Prayer is the most powerful gift He has given us to transform our schools. Establish a prayer group for your school with a humble heart for the sake of the children.

1:16 PM PRAYER

Please pray for the students who live in a turbulent neighborhood or home.

QUOTE FOR THE DAY

You can teach a student a lesson for a day; but if you can teach him to learn by creating curiosity, he will continue the learning process as long as he lives. **Clay P. Bedford**

NOTES:
_____
_____
_____
_____
_____

DAY 13

#iamachristianeducator

 Where we read the Bible with our brother and sisters in the public schools

DAILY PROMISES OF GOD
for educators

2ND CHRONICLES 20:20

NIV - *Early in the morning they left for the Desert of Tekoa. As they set out, Jehoshaphat stood and said, "Listen to me, Judah and people of Jerusalem! Have faith in the Lord your God and you will be upheld; have faith in his prophets and you will be successful."*

RSV - *And they rose early in the morning and went out into the wilderness of Teko'a; and as they went out, Jehosh'aphat stood and said, "Hear me, Judah and inhabitants of Jerusalem! Believe in the Lord your God, and you will be established; believe his prophets, and you will succeed."*

KJV - *And they rose early in the morning, and went forth into the wilderness of Tekoa: and as they went forth, Jehoshaphat stood and said, Hear me, O Judah, and ye inhabitants of Jerusalem; Believe in the Lord your God, so shall ye be established; believe his prophets, so shall ye prosper.*

LB - *Early the next morning the army of Judah went out into the wilderness of Tekoa. On the way Jehoshaphat stopped and called them to attention. "Listen to me, O people of Judah and Jerusalem," he said. "Believe in the Lord your God and you shall have success! Believe his prophets and everything will be all right!"*

NOTE TO THE EDUCATOR

Believe. **Believe** that God is with you right now. **Believe** that He can transform all things. **Believe** that He created all things. **Believe** that He has fearfully and wonderfully made each of your students and colleagues. **Believe** that He hears you when you pray. **Believe** that with His help all things are possible. **Believe** that He is the best thing that has ever happened to your school. **Believe** that there are other Christian brothers and sisters on your campus. **Believe.**

1:16 PM PRAYER

Please pray that our students have a teachable spirit all year long.

QUOTE FOR THE DAY

Keep away from people who try to belittle your ambitions. Small people always do that, but the really great make you feel that you, too, can become great. **Mark Twain**

NOTES:
_____
_____
_____
_____
_____

DAY 114

#iamachristianeducator

Where we read the Bible with our brother and sisters in the public schools

DAILY PROMISES OF GOD
for educators

PSALM 5:3

DAY 15

NIV - *In the morning, Lord, you hear my voice; in the morning I lay my requests before you and wait expectantly.*

RSV - *O Lord, in the morning thou dost hear my voice; in the morning I prepare a sacrifice for thee, and watch.*

KJV - *My voice shalt thou hear in the morning, O Lord; in the morning will I direct my prayer unto thee, and will look up.*

LB - *Each morning I will look to you in heaven and lay my requests before you, praying earnestly.*

NOTE TO THE EDUCATOR

Do you pray first thing in the morning? Is He your first thought? If not, experiment for the next 21 days by thanking Him the minute your eyes open. Praise Him with your first thoughts. Pray in the car as you come to school and pray the moment you arrive on campus. Pray when you walk down the hall. Pray when you enter your classroom or office. They tell us that it takes only 21 days to form a habit and this one is worth it because He hears your voice. It's a promise.

1:16 PM PRAYER

Please pray for the needs of the custodial staff at your school.

QUOTE FOR THE DAY

It is impossible for a man to learn what he thinks he already knows. **Epictetus**

NOTES:

_____
_____
_____
_____
_____

#iamachristianeducator

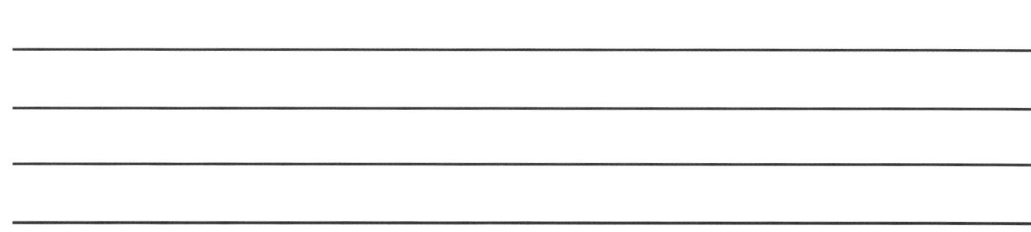

Where we read the Bible with our brother and sisters in the public schools

DAILY PROMISES OF GOD
for educators

PSALM 5:11-12

NIV - *But let all who take refuge in you be glad;*
let them ever sing for joy.
Spread your protection over them,
that those who love your name may rejoice in you.
Surely, Lord, you bless the righteous;
you surround them with your favor as with a shield.

RSV - *But let all who take refuge in thee rejoice,*
let them ever sing for joy;
and do thou defend them,
that those who love thy name may exult in thee.
For thou dost bless the righteous, O Lord;
thou dost cover him with favor as with a shield.

KJV - *But let all those that put their trust in thee rejoice: let them ever shout for joy, because thou defendest them: let them also that love thy name be joyful in thee. For thou, Lord, wilt bless the righteous; with favour wilt thou compass him as with a shield.*

LB - *But make everyone rejoice who puts his trust in you. Keep them shouting for joy because you are defending them. Fill all who love you with your happiness. For you bless the godly man, O Lord; you protect him with your shield of love.*

NOTE TO THE EDUCATOR

He protects us with His shield of love. Wow, that's beautiful! As Christians in the public school, we can protect our students with a shield of love. We love them because of His love. It is very difficult to love the unlovable, to love the students who are being disrespectful or rebellious, but that is our charge as a Christian. They will know us by our love. Let us pray for His love to cover us that we may protect our students with a shield of love.

1:16 PM PRAYER

Please pray for the needs of the school nurse.

QUOTE FOR THE DAY

Challenges are what make life interesting and overcoming them makes life meaningful.
Joshua Marine

NOTES:

_____
_____
_____
_____
_____

DAY 16

#iamachristianeducator

Where we read the Bible with our brother and sisters in the public schools

DAILY PROMISES OF GOD
for educators

PSALM 9:10

NIV - *Those who know your name trust in you,*
for you, Lord, have never forsaken those who seek you.

RSV - *And those who know thy name put their trust in thee,*
for thou, O Lord, hast not forsaken those who seek thee.

KJV - *And they that know thy name will put their trust in thee: for thou, Lord, hast not forsaken them that seek thee.*

LB - *All those who know your mercy, Lord, will count on you for help. For you have never yet forsaken those who trust in you.*

NOTE TO THE EDUCATOR

The Lord's name is the Name above all names. Knowing His Name is comfort and strength. When we open AW 180 each school day in prayer, we always do an ABC prayer of adoration together with a different name or description of Him for each letter of the alphabet. Have you tried doing that yet? It's a great way to come to know many of His incredible powers and gifts that He has given those who love Him. Try going around your prayer group one-by-one naming a characteristic or Name of God for each letter. Go all the way around the group until you complete all 26 letters. Trusting in His Name yields His faithfulness.

1:16 PM PRAYER

Please pray for the needs of our substitute teachers.

QUOTE FOR THE DAY

We can complain because rose bushes have thorns, or rejoice because thorn bushes have roses.
Abraham Lincoln

NOTES:

_____
_____
_____
_____
_____

DAY 17

#iamachristianeducator

Where we read the Bible with our brother and sisters in the public schools

DAILY PROMISES OF GOD
for educators

PSALM 12:7

DAY 18

NIV - *You, Lord, will keep the needy safe and will protect us forever from the wicked.*

RSV - *Do thou, O Lord, protect us, guard us ever from this generation.*

KJV - *Thou shalt keep them, O Lord, thou shalt preserve them from this generation for ever.*

LB - *O Lord, we know that you will forever preserve your own from the reach of evil men.*

NOTE TO THE EDUCATOR

We have a front row seat to the beauty and dilemma of the great experiment of public schools to educate EVERY child. Students who love to learn, students who can't learn, students who don't want to learn are our responsibility each day. Our public schools are a kaleidoscope of every family in America with every issue imaginable. As Christian educators we can take comfort in this promise that God will preserve all those who love Him through the generations into eternity. When problems seem insurmountable, pray the promises throughout the Bible for encouragement, truth and strength.

1:16 PM PRAYER

Please pray for the child who needs courage to take risks.

QUOTE FOR THE DAY

Life is like a box of chocolates. You never know what you're gonna get.   **Forrest Grump**

NOTES:

_____
_____
_____
_____
_____

#iamachristianeducator

Where we read the Bible with our brother and sisters in the public schools

DAILY PROMISES OF GOD
for educators

PSALM 23:1-2

NIV - *The Lord is my shepherd, I lack nothing. He makes me lie down in green pastures, he leads me beside quiet waters,*

RSV - *The Lord is my shepherd, I shall not want; he makes me lie down in green pastures. He leads me beside still waters;*

KJV - *The Lord is my shepherd; I shall not want. He maketh me to lie down in green pastures: he leadeth me beside the still waters.*

LB - *Because the Lord is my Shepherd, I have everything I need! He lets me rest in the meadow grass and leads me beside the quiet streams.*

NOTE TO THE EDUCATOR

What a beautiful picture of peace green pastures and quiet waters are! When the Lord is the Shepherd of our lives, that kind of peace is a promise. What is your classroom like? Is it peaceful or chaotic? With the model of our Lord, you are the shepherd of your classroom. You can create a safe place for your students where they are secure and lack nothing, a place of peace. Does it seem impossible? For us, yes. For Him all things are possible. Pray specifically for a safe classroom where the Shepherd can guide the shepherd of the classroom.

1:16 PM PRAYER

Please pray for the fallen heroes and their families of 9/11.

QUOTE FOR THE DAY

Some people look for a beautiful place, others make a place beautiful. - **Hazrat Inayat Khan**

NOTES:
_____
_____
_____
_____
_____

Where we read the Bible with our brother and sisters in the public schools

DAILY PROMISES OF GOD
for educators

PSALM 23:5

DAY 20

NIV - *You prepare a table before me in the presence of my enemies. You anoint my head with oil; my cup overflows.*

RSV - *Thou preparest a table before me in the presence of my enemies; thou anointest my head with oil, my cup overflows.*

KJV - *Thou preparest a table before me in the presence of mine enemies: thou anointest my head with oil; my cup runneth over.*

LB - *You provide delicious food for me in the presence of my enemies. You have welcomed me as your guest; blessings overflow!*

NOTE TO THE EDUCATOR

Want the solution to bullying? It is Ps. 23:5! If Christians young and old really believed this verse, we would stand bold on this incredible promise. As a Christian educator in the public schools, we cannot teach this Psalm devotionally, but when we live it out in our lives others will want to know what we have. Being a contagious Christian is appealing. Even our enemies will wonder what we have and will want a part of that kind of peace. We are a people who trust the Lord for each day in our public schools!

1:16 PM PRAYER

Please pray for any students who are hungry.

QUOTE FOR THE DAY

We cannot see our reflection in running water. It is only in still water we can see.
Taoist Proverb

NOTES:
_____
_____
_____
_____
_____

#iamachristianeducator

Where we read the Bible with our brother and sisters in the public schools

DAILY PROMISES OF GOD
for educators

PSALM 25:14

DAY 221

NIV - *The Lord confides in those who fear him; he makes his covenant known to them.*

RSV - *The friendship of the Lord is for those who fear him, and he makes known to them his covenant.*

KJV - *The secret of the Lord is with them that fear him; and he will shew them his covenant.*

LB - *Friendship with God is reserved for those who reverence him. With them alone he shares the secrets of his promises.*

NOTE TO THE EDUCATOR

The Lord is our friend. That is an unfathomable statement, even a bit disrespectful when you don't know the Lord. God is clearly promising His friendship to us when we fear Him. How can fear and friendship possibly go together? Awe may be a more understandable word than fear, but nonetheless, we stand in awe that the God of the universe has time for us and makes known to us the hope of His promises. No matter how hard your day in school is today, you can rest in the promise of His friendship and love.

1:16 PM PRAYER

Please pray that our school boards make wise decisions for our school communities.

QUOTE FOR THE DAY

A little consideration, a little thought for others, makes all the difference.
A.A. Milne, Winnie the Pooh

NOTES:
_____
_____
_____
_____
_____

#iamachristianeducator

Where we read the Bible with our brother and sisters in the public schools

DAILY PROMISES OF GOD
for educators

PSALM 27:14

NIV - *Wait for the Lord; be strong and take heart and wait for the Lord.*

RSV - *Wait for the Lord; be strong, and let your heart take courage; yea, wait for the Lord!*

KJV - *Wait on the Lord: be of good courage, and he shall strengthen thine heart: wait, I say, on the Lord.*

LB - *Don't be impatient. Wait for the Lord, and he will come and save you! Be brave, stouthearted, and courageous. Yes, wait and he will help you.*

NOTE TO THE EDUCATOR

Isn't it just like us to want to rush God? We pray for a few days and don't think He's listening or doesn't have time for us? Or we rush away the days, weeks and whole school year to get to summer. The Lord is patient and does not work according to our calendars and schedules. Learning to wait on the Lord is one of the hardest things to do but has great rewards.
Every time we ask our students to be patient when they don't understand why they have to study something, think of your own desires that seem to be taking forever. He is steadfast and immovable and ever abounding in love for you in His time and way.

1:16 PM PRAYER

Please pray for a colleague who is being observed in the near future.

QUOTE FOR THE DAY

Eighty percent of success is showing up. **Woody Allen**

NOTES:

_____
_____
_____
_____
_____

DAY 222

#iamachristianeducator

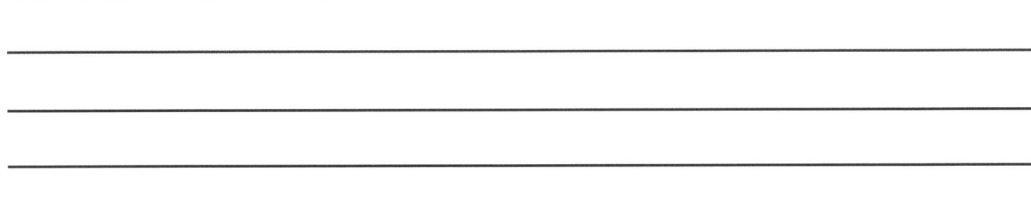
Where we read the Bible with our brother and sisters in the public schools

DAILY PROMISES OF GOD
for educators

PSALM 30:5

NIV - *For his anger lasts only a moment, but his favor lasts a lifetime; weeping may stay for the night, but rejoicing comes in the morning.*

RSV - *For his anger is but for a moment, and his favor is for a lifetime. Weeping may tarry for the night, but joy comes with the morning.*

KJV - *For his anger endureth but a moment; in his favour is life: weeping may endure for a night, but joy cometh in the morning.*

LB - *His anger lasts a moment; his favor lasts for life! Weeping may go on all night, but in the morning there is joy.*

NOTE TO THE EDUCATOR

There's nothing like getting a fresh start. We are most unique in education because we get a fresh start each school year: new students, new colleagues, new administrators, new curriculum and standards, etc. What a blessing. We start the year off with high expectations and enthusiasm for the possibilities and somehow as the year progresses some of that newness wears off. The Lord affords us the same opportunity each day! No matter what has happened today, we are renewed each morning. What joy He provides. As Christian educators let us make sure we extend that same favor to our students and give them the opportunity to start fresh each new day. The spirit of joy will fill our classrooms as we model His favor for us to them.

1:16 PM PRAYER

Please pray for wisdom in time management for our colleagues and students.

QUOTE FOR THE DAY

If you judge people, you have no time to love them. **Mother Teresa**

NOTES:
_____
_____
_____
_____
_____

Where we read the Bible with our brother and sisters in the public schools

DAILY PROMISES OF GOD
for educators

PSALM 30:11

DAY 24

NIV - *You turned my wailing into dancing; you removed my sackcloth and clothed me with joy.*

RSV - *Thou hast turned for me my mourning into dancing; thou hast loosed my sackcloth and girded me with gladness.*

KJV - *Thou hast turned for me my mourning into dancing: thou hast put off my sackcloth, and girded me with gladness.*

LB - *Then he turned my sorrow into joy! He took away my clothes of mourning and clothed me with joy.*

NOTE TO THE EDUCATOR

Be comforted dear one who has sorrow. How do our non-Christian friends and students ever deal with sorrow without the Lord? For with the Lord we have His never ending love and comfort. He turns sorrow into gladness! Trust Him, He can help anyone who believes He can change all things. How do we help our students with great sorrow? It's a very difficult time to be an educator when one of our students or colleagues is experiencing great sorrow. We know that we must be Jesus to them. Pray for them. Give them comfort. Listen to them and most of all turn their sorrow over to God that He may turn it into dancing. It's His promise to those who believe.

1:16 PM PRAYER

Please pray for the students in your school that have lost a parent.

QUOTE FOR THE DAY

The only thing worse than being blind is having sight but no vision. **Helen Keller**

NOTES:

_____
_____
_____
_____
_____

#iamachristianeducator

Where we read the Bible with our brother and sisters in the public schools

DAILY PROMISES OF GOD
for educators

PSALM 32:8

NIV - *I will instruct you and teach you in the way you should go; I will counsel you with my loving eye on you.*

RSV - *I will instruct you and teach you the way you should go; I will counsel you with my eye upon you.*

KJV - *I will instruct thee and teach thee in the way which thou shalt go: I will guide thee with mine eye.*

LB - *I will instruct you (says the Lord) and guide you along the best pathway for your life; I will advise you and watch your progress.*

NOTE TO THE EDUCATOR

The Lord's loving eye is upon us each and every day, each and every moment. In a classroom, we have a loving eye guiding and instructing our students in the way that they should go. It reminds me of the myth of teachers having eyes behind their heads. That kind of with-it-ness is a gift. When it comes from love, the students are able to trust us because they know we have their best interest at heart. What a privilege it is to know that our God has the Ultimate With-it-ness as He counsels, instructs, teaches, and advises us in the way that we should go. This promise is an incredible model for us to emulate for the love of our students.

1:16 PM PRAYER

Please pray for the student who consistently does not do his or her assignments.

QUOTE FOR THE DAY

Not all of us can do great things. But we can do small things with great love. **Mother Teresa**

NOTES:

_____

_____

_____

_____

_____

Where we read the Bible with our brother and sisters in the public schools

DAY 25

#iamachristianeducator

DAILY PROMISES OF GOD
for educators

PSALM 36:6-7

NIV - *Your righteousness is like the highest mountains, your justice like the great deep. You, Lord, preserve both people and animals. How priceless is your unfailing love, O God! People take refuge in the shadow of your wings.*

RSV - *Thy righteousness is like the mountains of God, thy judgments are like the great deep; man and beast thou savest, O Lord. How precious is thy steadfast love, O God! The children of men take refuge in the shadow of thy wings.*

KJV - *Thy righteousness is like the great mountains; thy judgments are a great deep: O Lord, thou preservest man and beast. How excellent is thy lovingkindness, O God! therefore the children of men put their trust under the shadow of thy wings.*

LB - *Your justice is as solid as God's mountains. Your decisions are as full of wisdom as the oceans are with water. You are concerned for men and animals alike. How precious is your constant love, O God! All humanity takes refuge in the shadow of your wings.*

NOTE TO THE EDUCATOR

Higher than high, greater than great is the love of the Lord for His children. Ours is a high calling because we have charge and influence over the next generation. Ours is a high calling because we have to answer to the One Whose righteousness is higher than the highest mountain and deeper than the deepest sea. Let us thank the Lord that He has given all of us refuge under the shadow of His wings. How precious and priceless is the love of God for His children.

1:16 PM PRAYER

Please pray for a colleague who is struggling with family issues.

QUOTE FOR THE DAY

For God has not given us a spirit of fear, but of power and of love and of a sound mind.
2 Timothy 1:7

NOTES:

_____
_____
_____
_____
_____

DAY 26

#iamachristianeducator

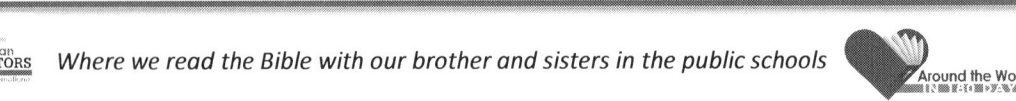

Where we read the Bible with our brother and sisters in the public schools

DAILY PROMISES OF GOD
for educators

PSALM 37:4

NIV - *Take delight in the Lord, and he will give you the desires of your heart.*

RSV - *Take delight in the Lord, and he will give you the desires of your heart.*

KJV - *Delight thyself also in the Lord: and he shall give thee the desires of thine heart.*

LB - *Be delighted with the Lord. Then he will give you all your heart's desires.*

NOTE TO THE EDUCATOR

Do you delight in the Lord? What does that mean? Do you seek Him for all your needs? Do you give Him thanks for the good days and even the bad days in school? Do you ask Him to help your students and colleagues to be successful? Do you think about Him? Does He give you great pleasure? Delighting in the Lord is trusting and knowing that He has created you to be an educator and that He will give you all the desires of your heart when you delight in Him. As we delight in Him, we will learn how to delight in our students also, even and perhaps especially, those who don't deserve our love. Be delighted in all that you do. It's contagious.

1:16 PM PRAYER

Please pray for local churches to pray for and/or adopt our schools.

QUOTE FOR THE DAY

In order to succeed, we must first believe that we can. **Nikos Kazantzakis**

NOTES:
_____
_____
_____
_____
_____

Where we read the Bible with our brother and sisters in the public schools

DAILY PROMISES OF GOD
for educators

PSALM 37:18

NIV - *The blameless spend their days under the Lord's care, and their inheritance will endure forever.*

RSV - *The Lord knows the days of the blameless, and their heritage will abide for ever.*

KJV - *The Lord knoweth the days of the upright: and their inheritance shall be for ever.*

LB - *Day by day the Lord observes the good deeds done by godly men, and gives them eternal rewards.*

NOTE TO THE EDUCATOR

It's very difficult to think about eternity when we are in the middle of a hectic school day. I know that I couldn't even find a moment to make a phone call. It's just the nature of education. We give it our all, all day long and live a very myopic routine at times. Why not pause and think about eternity? We serve a mighty God Who has placed us in the public schools to minister to our students and colleagues that they may see Jesus in us. We need no words to be Jesus with skin on, but we are His hands and ears and eyes and heart to those we impact each day. Stop and think about that during the day when you are feeling unimportant. We are under His care and empowered by His love. Our reward is eternity with Him!

1:16 PM PRAYER

Please pray for students whose parents are divorced or separated.

QUOTE FOR THE DAY

The real gift of gratitude is that the more grateful you are, the more present you become.
Robert Holden

NOTES:

_____

_____

_____

_____

_____

DAY 228

#iamachristianeducator

Where we read the Bible with our brother and sisters in the public schools

DAILY PROMISES OF GOD
for educators

PSALM 37:23-24

NIV - *The Lord makes firm the steps of the one who delights in him; though he may stumble, he will not fall, for the Lord upholds him with his hand.*

RSV - *The steps of a man are from the Lord, and he establishes him in whose way he delights; though he fall, he shall not be cast headlong, for the Lord is the stay of his hand.*

KJV - *The steps of a good man are ordered by the Lord: and he delighteth in his way. Though he fall, he shall not be utterly cast down: for the Lord upholdeth him with his hand.*

LB - *The steps of good men are directed by the Lord. He delights in each step they take. If they fall, it isn't fatal, for the Lord holds them with his hand.*

NOTE TO THE EDUCATOR

So you had a bad day. Did you know that we all have those kind of days occasionally? Don't give up. If your students did not respond the way you wanted today, tomorrow you get another chance. Don't give up. If that lesson that you worked so hard to prepare was insufficient, you get an opportunity to fix it and do it better. Don't give up. If you disciplined a student too harshly, let them know. Apologize and ask for forgiveness. Don't give up. We serve a beautiful God Who will never let us go. He holds us up. He has promised to uphold us with His mighty hand. Don't give up. You will be glad you persevered.

1:16 PM PRAYER

Please pray for student and staff safety as they travel to and from school.

QUOTE FOR THE DAY

The strongest people are not those who show strength in front of us but those who win battles we know nothing about. **Unknown author**

NOTES:

_____
_____
_____
_____
_____

DAY 29

#iamachristianeducator

 Where we read the Bible with our brother and sisters in the public schools

DAILY PROMISES OF GOD
for educators

PSALM 40:1

DAY 30

NIV - *I waited patiently for the Lord; he turned to me and heard my cry.*

RSV - *I waited patiently for the Lord; he inclined to me and heard my cry.*

KJV - *I waited patiently for the Lord; and he inclined unto me, and heard my cry.*

LB - *I waited patiently for God to help me; then he listened and heard my cry.*

NOTE TO THE EDUCATOR

Sometimes we pray for something for a long time and it seems like God is not listening. He is always listening to us. He knows our requests even before we ask, yet at times it seems that our prayers are unanswered. Waiting is not a practice that most of us enjoy and waiting patiently is seemingly impossible at times. Yet as we look back on our lives' requests, we can see that He is a "just in time" God Who not only listens to our cries but inclines Himself toward us. Hindsight is 20/20 and gives us the chance to witness what God has done in our lives. If you are not already journaling, I highly recommend a small daily journal where you record your blessings large and small each week. Be sure to date the entries and look back each school year. You will be amazed at just how attentive He has been to the cries of your heart.

1:16 PM PRAYER

Please pray for a sense of gratitude.

QUOTE FOR THE DAY

Life is 10% what happens to me and 90% of how I react to it. **Charles Swindle**

NOTES:

_____

_____

_____

_____

_____

#iamachristianeducator

Where we read the Bible with our brother and sisters in the public schools

DAILY PROMISES OF GOD
for educators

PSALM 46:1

DAY 31

NIV - *God is our refuge and strength, an ever-present help in trouble.*

RSV - *God is our refuge and strength, a very present help in trouble.*

KJV - *God is our refuge and strength, a very present help in trouble.*

LB - *God is our refuge and strength, a tested help in times of trouble.*

NOTE TO THE EDUCATOR

Getting in trouble and having troubles are a part of school life. Administrators, teachers and paraprofessionals have to deal with student troubles all day, every day. What are troubles that affect educators? Health, financial, mental, spiritual, and all the humankind issues that can be found anywhere else are a part of our public school each day. The only way to truly solve troubles is to go to the One Who can solve them. Our God has promised that He is our refuge. We can hide in Him and have a place of safety. He is our Strength when we have none and He is ever present, no matter when or where our troubles occur.

1:16 PM PRAYER

Please pray for any student or colleague with a loved one suffering from a terminal illness.

QUOTE FOR THE DAY

Discovery lies not in seeking new lands but in seeking with new eyes. **Marcel Proust**

NOTES:
_____
_____
_____
_____
_____

#iamachristianeducator

Where we read the Bible with our brother and sisters in the public schools

DAILY PROMISES OF GOD
for educators

PSALM 46:10

NIV - *He says, "Be still, and know that I am God; I will be exalted among the nations, I will be exalted in the earth."*

RSV - *"Be still, and know that I am God. I am exalted among the nations, I am exalted in the earth!"*

KJV - *Be still, and know that I am God: I will be exalted among the heathen, I will be exalted in the earth.*

LB - *"Stand silent! Know that I am God! I will be honored by every nation in the world!"*

NOTE TO THE EDUCATOR

Being exalted eternally is reserved for God and His incredible coming, but did you know that educators are in an exalted position? As a member of this highly regarded profession, we must uphold in the way we conduct ourselves, the way we speak to others and the way we walk our walk. In the public schools, educators are disallowed from praying in front of the room, yet we maintain the First Amendment right to pray privately or with our peers. In order to establish and maintain our high calling, we need prayer. We need His help as we represent Him. Let us find time in the school day to be still and know that He is God.

1:16 PM PRAYER

Please pray to display the joy of the Lord.

QUOTE FOR THE DAY

Life is like riding a bicycle. To keep your balance you must keep moving. **Albert Einstein**

NOTES:
___
___
___
___
___

DAY 32

#iamachristianeducator

Where we read the Bible with our brother and sisters in the public schools

DAILY PROMISES OF GOD
for educators

PSALM 56:11

DAY 333

NIV - *In God I trust and am not afraid. What can man do to me?*

RSV - *In God I trust without a fear. What can man do to me?*

KJV - *In God have I put my trust: I will not be afraid what man can do unto me.*

LB - *I am trusting God—oh, praise his promises! I am not afraid of anything mere man can do to me! Yes, praise his promises.*

NOTE TO THE EDUCATOR

The official motto of the United States is "In God We Trust." How many of those signs do you see in your school? It is legal and appropriate to post and teach our national motto to the next generation. Look on our paper money and coins and you will find "In God We Trust" also. More than posting, mentioning or referring to this motto, what does it say to us as Christian educators? No matter what obstacles we face, whatever difficulties confront us in our daily school lives, there is nothing that man can bring against us that is bigger than our Great God of promises. Let us trust Him wholeheartedly and praise Him for His love for our brothers and sisters in the public schools for the good of all our students.

1:16 PM PRAYER

Please praise God for His faithfulness.

QUOTE FOR THE DAY

Two roads diverged in a wood, and I—I took the one less traveled by, And that has made all the difference. **Robert Frost**

NOTES:
_____
_____
_____
_____
_____

Where we read the Bible with our brother and sisters in the public schools

#iamachristianeducator

DAILY PROMISES OF GOD
for educators

PSALM 68:5

DAY 34

NIV - *A father to the fatherless, a defender of widows, is God in his holy dwelling.*

RSV - *Father of the fatherless and protector of widows is God in his holy habitation.*

KJV - *A father of the fatherless, and a judge of the widows, is God in his holy habitation.*

LB - *He is a father to the fatherless; he gives justice to the widows, for he is holy.*

NOTE TO THE EDUCATOR

Do you have any students who have lost a parent? It is possible that you don't even know. Try to find out if any of your students are fatherless or have lost a mother. There is no need to tell the student(s) once you find out, but begin to pray for their hearts, their home life and their relationship with God. He is the Father to the fatherless. Make special effort to be loving to these children for their lives are much more tender with such a great loss. Consider adopting one of them academically by checking in with them a little more often than you would with other students just to see how they are doing with their grades. Become his/her official mentor and be God's agent and protector this year for some of the weaker among our children.

1:16 PM PRAYER

Please pray for the Christ followers in our schools who are staff, parents and students.

QUOTE FOR THE DAY

Don't be pushed by your problems. Be led by your dreams. **Ralph Waldo Emerson**

NOTES:

_____
_____
_____
_____
_____

#iamachristianeducator

Where we read the Bible with our brother and sisters in the public schools

DAILY PROMISES OF GOD
for educators **PSALM 68:19**

DAY 35

NIV - *Praise be to the Lord, to God our Savior, who daily bears our burdens.*

RSV - *Blessed be the Lord, who daily bears us up; God is our salvation.*

KJV - *Blessed be the Lord, who daily loadeth us with benefits, even the God of our salvation. Selah.*

LB - *What a glorious Lord! He who daily bears our burdens also gives us our salvation.*

NOTE TO THE EDUCATOR

There are many burdens to being an educator: students that have learning disabilities, disgruntled parents, new curriculum and standards, deadlines and all the human factors. Brothers and sisters! We have the Lord, our God Who bears our burdens. Don't take them all on yourself. Let Him bear them. What a gift. I love how the KJV doesn't even mention burdens, but instead describes His action as "daily loadeth us with benefits." As Christ followers, we have the distinct benefit of casting our burdens upon Him because He cares for us. Don't take on any unnecessary burdens when the Lord of the universe has already bore it all for us.

1:16 PM PRAYER

Please pray that our paraprofessionals are appreciated.

QUOTE FOR THE DAY

The greatest use of a life is to spend it on something that will outlast it. **William James**

NOTES:
_____
_____
_____
_____
_____

#iamachristianeducator

Where we read the Bible with our brother and sisters in the public schools

DAILY PROMISES OF GOD
for educators

PSALM 84:11

NIV - *For the Lord God is a sun and shield; the Lord bestows favor and honor; no good thing does he withhold from those whose walk is blameless.*

RSV - *For the Lord God is a sun and shield; he bestows favor and honor. No good thing does the Lord withhold from those who walk uprightly.*

KJV - *For the Lord God is a sun and shield: the Lord will give grace and glory: no good thing will he withhold from them that walk uprightly.*

LB - *For Jehovah God is our Light and our Protector. He gives us grace and glory. No good thing will he withhold from those who walk along his paths.*

NOTE TO THE EDUCATOR

Being is an educator is a high calling because we are living out our faith as we walk our walk. We don't talk about Jesus to our students, but we show Jesus in all that we do. We are His ambassadors in the public schools. Our Father bestows favor on us as we walk this walk. We are not alone. There is beauty in unity. Find another Christian educator and pray regularly with them for the needs of your school. As you walk along His paths, it is His promise that He will be a sun and shield for you. He will withhold no good thing from you and He will bestow favor and honor. Praises to our God of grace and glory.

1:16 PM PRAYER

Please pray for any students that may have recently lost a pet.

QUOTE FOR THE DAY

Do the best you can until you know better. Then when you know better, do better.
Maya Angelou

NOTES:

_____
_____
_____
_____
_____

DAY 36

#iamachristianeducator

Where we read the Bible with our brother and sisters in the public schools

DAILY PROMISES OF GOD
for educators

PSALM 86:7

NIV - *When I am in distress, I call to you, because you answer me.*

RSV - *In the day of my trouble I call on thee, for thou dost answer me.*

KJV - *In the day of my trouble I will call upon thee: for thou wilt answer me.*

LB - *I will call to you whenever trouble strikes, and you will help me.*

NOTE TO THE EDUCATOR

God promises that He will answer us as we call on Him whenever trouble comes. I wonder if anyone has ever had a trouble-free school year? Pretty silly, huh? Is your immediate reaction to call on God for help when trouble happens? If you are a Christian educator, you have an assurance that He will help you, that He will hear your cry and He will answer. It takes belief and practice. There is no trouble too small. There is nothing He can't solve. Let's make a habit of calling out to Him for all our troubles, big and small, and watch Him transform our school and personal lives.

1:16 PM PRAYER

Please pray for the ability to refrain from grumbling.

QUOTE FOR THE DAY

Nothing great was ever achieved without enthusiasm. **Ralph Waldo Emerson**

NOTES:
_____
_____
_____
_____
_____

DAY 37

#iamachristianeducator

Where we read the Bible with our brother and sisters in the public schools

DAILY PROMISES OF GOD
for educators

PSALM 91:1-2

NIV - *Whoever dwells in the shelter of the Most High will rest in the shadow of the Almighty. I will say of the Lord, "He is my refuge and my fortress, my God, in whom I trust."*

RSV - *He who dwells in the shelter of the Most High, who abides in the shadow of the Almighty, will say to the Lord, "My refuge and my fortress; my God, in whom I trust."*

KJV - *He that dwelleth in the secret place of the most High shall abide under the shadow of the Almighty. I will say of the Lord, He is my refuge and my fortress: my God; in him will I trust.*

LB - *We live within the shadow of the Almighty, sheltered by the God who is above all gods. This I declare, that he alone is my refuge, my place of safety; he is my God, and I am trusting him.*

NOTE TO THE EDUCATOR

There is rest in the shadow of the Lord. I wonder if you rest. Do you take dedicated time to rest from the never-ending school work? Do you take time to stay off your devices? Do you take time to read the Word and dwell in His presence? If not, you are missing out on one of the greatest benefits of being a child of God. Begin with a small time period. Increase your rest time and place boundaries around it. Let nothing interfere with your Sabbath time with God. He designed rest as one of the essential benefits to your Christian walk. He can be heard a lot better when all the distractions are laid aside. Trust Him and rest in Him.

1:16 PM PRAYER

Please pray that the Lord will help us to love the unlovable.

QUOTE FOR THE DAY

Believe you can and you're halfway there. **Theodore Roosevelt**

NOTES:

_____
_____
_____
_____
_____

Where we read the Bible with our brother and sisters in the public schools

DAILY PROMISES OF GOD
for educators

PSALM 91:7

DAY 339

NIV - *A thousand may fall at your side, ten thousand at your right hand, but it will not come near you.*

RSV - *A thousand may fall at your side, ten thousand at your right hand; but it will not come near you.*

KJV - *A thousand shall fall at thy side, and ten thousand at thy right hand; but it shall not come nigh thee.*

LB - *Though a thousand fall at my side, though ten thousand are dying around me, the evil will not touch me.*

NOTE TO THE EDUCATOR

There are times when our colleagues wonder how we could possibly remain positive when everyone else is disgruntled. That is Christ in us. Other times they notice that we are serving our students and colleagues behind the scenes not looking for recognition. That is Christ in us. Perhaps we are perceived as different. That is Christ in us. Being a contagious Christian, having something that others want is our way of telling others about our Lord and Savior. May God help you to be always aware of Christ in you, Christ around you, Christ in front of you, Christ in back of you, and Christ above you in order to give Him the glory and help others come to know Him as we do.

1:16 PM PRAYER

Please pray to be humble. (Phil. 2:3)

QUOTE FOR THE DAY

Travel light, live light, spread the light, be the light. **Yogi Bhajan**

NOTES:
_____
_____
_____
_____
_____

#iamachristianeducator

Where we read the Bible with our brother and sisters in the public schools

DAILY PROMISES OF GOD
for educators

PSALM 91:15-16

NIV - *He will call on me, and I will answer him; I will be with him in trouble, I will deliver him and honor him. With long life I will satisfy him and show him my salvation.*

RSV - *When he calls to me, I will answer him; I will be with him in trouble, I will rescue him and honor him. With long life I will satisfy him, and show him my salvation.*

KJV - *He shall call upon me, and I will answer him: I will be with him in trouble; I will deliver him, and honour him. With long life will I satisfy him, and shew him my salvation.*

LB - *When he calls on me, I will answer; I will be with him in trouble and rescue him and honor him. I will satisfy him with a full life and give him my salvation.*

NOTE TO THE EDUCATOR

Jesus is the One Who satisfies. No matter what our situation is in public school, there is satisfaction in Him. Are you praying for a better class? Be satisfied in Him. He will help you. Are you praying for a way to get through this year? Be satisfied in Him. His grace is sufficient. You don't have to get out of your situation, you need to address it with His help. He is always ready. He calls to us, delivers us, honors us, rescues us and satisfies us with salvation through Him alone. He is with you today as He is everyday.

1:16 PM PRAYER

Please pray that we remember to put on the full armor of God (Eph. 6:10-17)

QUOTE FOR THE DAY

Spread love wherever you go. Let no one ever come to you without leaving happier.
  Mother Theresa

NOTES:

_____
_____
_____
_____
_____

DAY 40

#iamachristianeducator

Where we read the Bible with our brother and sisters in the public schools

DAILY PROMISES OF GOD
for educators

PSALM 94:14

DAY 141

NIV - *For the Lord will not reject his people; he will never forsake his inheritance.*

RSV - *For the Lord will not forsake his people; he will not abandon his heritage;*

KJV - *For the Lord will not cast off his people, neither will he forsake his inheritance.*

LB - *The Lord will not forsake his people, for they are his prize.*

NOTE TO THE EDUCATOR

You are His inheritance, His prize! As educators, we are not supposed to have favorites, but there are those few students that you can't help but favor. They tend to be our "prize" students. Have you ever thought about the idea that you are God's "prize" student? Only God can have more than one prize student and pull it off. Be encouraged each and every day that we serve a God Who is generous, kind and gentle. He is faithful, joyful and peaceful and He will never abandon us. We are won by His love and we serve in the public schools out of a grateful heart. May God bless what you do to His glory, so that your colleagues and students will also be blessed by you.

1:16 PM PRAYER

Please pray for the needs of the assistant principals.

QUOTE FOR THE DAY

The shortest distance between a problem and a solution is the distance between your knees and the floor. **Charles Stanley**

NOTES:
_____
_____
_____
_____
_____

#iamachristianeducator

Where we read the Bible with our brother and sisters in the public schools

DAILY PROMISES OF GOD
for educators

PSALM 97:10

DAY 42

NIV - *Let those who love the Lord hate evil, for he guards the lives of his faithful ones and delivers them from the hand of the wicked.*

RSV - *The Lord loves those who hate evil; he preserves the lives of his saints; he delivers them from the hand of the wicked.*

KJV - *Ye that love the Lord, hate evil: he preserveth the souls of his saints; he delivereth them out of the hand of the wicked.*

LB - *The Lord loves those who hate evil; he protects the lives of his people and rescues them from the wicked.*

NOTE TO THE EDUCATOR

Educators are protectors. We would not allow any evil to harm our students whether it comes from bullying or outside forces. To the best of our ability, we will protect and defend our students from harm. The Lord provides that protection for us. As we learn to love Him more each day, we understand how to hate evil. Darkness has no place in the public schools and only His light can truly invade the darkness. You have been placed in your school as an agent of light to shine His love and by it, protect your students. Go to Him first when you need to be the protector.

1:16 PM PRAYER

Please pray for forgiveness.

QUOTE FOR THE DAY

For what does it profit a man, if he gains the whole world yet loses his own soul? **(Luke 9:25)**

NOTES:
_____
_____
_____
_____
_____

#iamachristianeducator

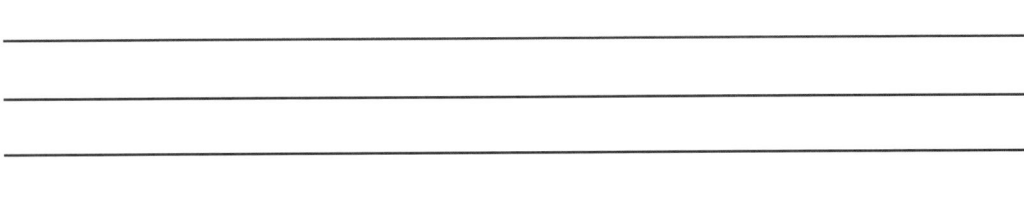
Where we read the Bible with our brother and sisters in the public schools

DAILY PROMISES OF GOD
for educators

PSALM 100:5

NIV - *For the Lord is good and his love endures forever; his faithfulness continues through all generations.*

RSV - *For the Lord is good; his steadfast love endures for ever, and his faithfulness to all generations.*

KJV - *For the Lord is good; his mercy is everlasting; and his truth endureth to all generations.*

LB - *For the Lord is always good. He is always loving and kind, and his faithfulness goes on and on to each succeeding generation.*

NOTE TO THE EDUCATOR

The Lord is good. He doesn't need our help to touch the next generation, yet He uses us as ambassadors to display His faithfulness. We are the Body of Christ in the public schools. As we walk each and every one of our campuses, He walks with us. Where there are Christian brothers and sisters, He is there also. He is faithful and will continue to each succeeding generation. It's a promise! Go out of your way today to be good to someone and do it for Christ's sake.

1:16 PM PRAYER

Please pray that we remember to begin each day in the Word of God and in prayer.

QUOTE FOR THE DAY

The most difficult thing is the decision to act, the rest is merely tenacity. **Amelia Earhart**

NOTES:

_____
_____
_____
_____
_____

Where we read the Bible with our brother and sisters in the public schools

DAILY PROMISES OF GOD
for educators

PSALM 103:1-5

NIV - *Praise the Lord, my soul; all my inmost being, praise his holy name. Praise the Lord, my soul, and forget not all his benefits— who forgives all your sins and heals all your diseases, who redeems your life from the pit and crowns you with love and compassion, who satisfies your desires with good things so that your youth is renewed like the eagle's.*

RSV - *Bless the Lord, O my soul; and all that is within me, bless his holy name! Bless the Lord, O my soul, and forget not all his benefits, who forgives all your iniquity, who heals all your diseases, who redeems your life from the Pit, who crowns you with steadfast love and mercy, who satisfies you with good as long as you live so that your youth is renewed like the eagle's.*

KJV - *Bless the Lord, O my soul: and all that is within me, bless his holy name. Bless the Lord, O my soul, and forget not all his benefits: Who forgiveth all thine iniquities; who healeth all thy diseases; Who redeemeth thy life from destruction; who crowneth thee with lovingkindness and tender mercies; Who satisfieth thy mouth with good things; so that thy youth is renewed like the eagle's.*

LB - *I bless the holy name of God with all my heart. Yes, I will bless the Lord and not forget the glorious things he does for me. He forgives all my sins. He heals me. He ransoms me from hell. He surrounds me with loving-kindness and tender mercies. He fills my life with good things! My youth is renewed like the eagle's!*

NOTE TO THE EDUCATOR

And forget not all His benefits! What a gift! Have you ever realized that there are benefits to being a Christian educator? The benefit package includes: forgiveness, healing, redemption, love, compassion, satisfaction, and renewal. What a tender-hearted, merciful God we serve. Praise Him today for His endless love and benefit package greater than any school board could ever offer.

1:16 PM PRAYER

Please pray for the student who is discouraged in his/her schoolwork.

QUOTE FOR THE DAY

Mankind must put an end to war — or war will put an end to mankind. **John F. Kennedy**

NOTES:

_____

_____

_____

_____

_____

DAY 444

#iamachristianeducator

 Where we read the Bible with our brother and sisters in the public schools

DAILY PROMISES OF GOD
for educators

PSALM 103:6

DAY 45

NIV - *The Lord works righteousness and justice for all the oppressed.*

RSV - *The Lord works vindication and justice for all who are oppressed.*

KJV - *The Lord executeth righteousness and judgment for all that are oppressed.*

LB - *He gives justice to all who are treated unfairly.*

NOTE TO THE EDUCATOR

Have you ever seen the Disney movie, "Hunchback of Notre Dame?" There is a beautiful song called, "God Help the Outcast," which reminds me of this verse. We have many students who are outcasts and we can be their greatest source of prayer, counseling and encouragement. For most of us that doesn't come naturally, but with Jesus Christ living in us, all things are made possible. Make an effort to seek out the outcast among your students and give them special opportunities to get to know you. Be contagious for Christ.

1:16 PM PRAYER

Please pray that we make the best use of our time. (Eph. 5:16)

QUOTE FOR THE DAY

A grateful person is rich in contentment.   **David Bednar**

NOTES:

_____
_____
_____
_____
_____

#iamachristianeducator

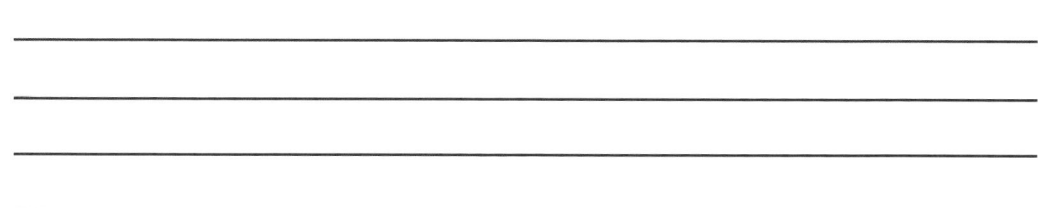

Where we read the Bible with our brother and sisters in the public schools

DAILY PROMISES OF GOD
for educators

PSALM 103:11-12

DAY 46

NIV - *For as high as the heavens are above the earth, so great is his love for those who fear him; as far as the east is from the west, so far has he removed our transgressions from us.*

RSV - *For as the heaven is high above the earth, so great is his mercy toward them that fear him. As far as the east is from the west, so far hath he removed our transgressions from us.*

KJV - *For as the heaven is high above the earth, so great is his mercy toward them that fear him. As far as the east is from the west, so far hath he removed our transgressions from us.*

LB - *For his mercy toward those who fear and honor him is as great as the height of the heavens above the earth. He has removed our sins as far away from us as the east is from the west.*

NOTE TO THE EDUCATOR

Can your wrap your mind around these verses? He loves beyond the scope of our understanding. He has removed our sins further than east is from the west. Have you tried to imagine how far east is from the west? If you start in one end you can never reach the other. If you try to go as high as the heavens are above the earth, you will never reach the end. He is vastness and intricacy. He is beyond our ability to comprehend, yet He promises to love us and even gives us the opportunity to pray. Let us give Him thanks today for His ever-abounding gifts.

1:16 PM PRAYER

Please pray for any student who has a loved one in prison.

QUOTE FOR THE DAY

Be filled with wonder, be touched by peace. **Unknown**

NOTES:
_____
_____
_____
_____
_____

#iamachristianeducator

 Where we read the Bible with our brother and sisters in the public schools

DAILY PROMISES OF GOD
for educators

PSALM 103:13

NIV - *As a father has compassion on his children, so the Lord has compassion on those who fear him.*

RSV - *As a father pities his children, so the Lord pities those who fear him.*

KJV - *Like as a father pitieth his children, so the Lord pitieth them that fear him.*

LB - *He is like a father to us, tender and sympathetic to those who reverence him.*

NOTE TO THE EDUCATOR

Our role as Christ-follower is to be like Him. We have the awesome calling to be His ears and eyes and a gentle touch in our schools. One of His most precious attributes is compassion. He is tender and sympathetic and there is never any doubt that He will be faithful. How is our compassionate meter in the classroom? Does it rise high when our students are acting up? Is it possible that many of their disrespectful ways are manifested because they are hurting and it really has nothing to do with us? Try a little compassion the next time you need to discipline a student. Take them outside your door and speak to them with grace and let Jesus with skin on handle the confrontation.

1:16 PM PRAYER

Please pray that students be respectful to adults and their peers.

QUOTE FOR THE DAY

Setting goals is the first step in turning the invisible into the visible. **Tony Robbins**

NOTES:

_____
_____
_____
_____
_____

DAY 47

#iamachristianeducator

Where we read the Bible with our brother and sisters in the public schools

DAILY PROMISES OF GOD
for educators
PSALM 116:5-6

NIV - *The Lord is gracious and righteous; our God is full of compassion. The Lord protects the unwary; when I was brought low, he saved me.*

RSV - *Gracious is the Lord, and righteous; our God is merciful. The Lord preserves the simple; when I was brought low, he saved me.*

KJV - *Gracious is the Lord, and righteous; yea, our God is merciful. The Lord preserveth the simple: I was brought low, and he helped me.*

LB - *How kind he is! How good he is! So merciful, this God of ours! The Lord protects the simple and the childlike; I was facing death, and then he saved me*

NOTE TO THE EDUCATOR

What does grace look like in the classroom? Grace defined is: **G**od's **R**iches **A**t **C**hrist's **E**xpense. He paid it all. He gave all. As Christian educators, we need to keep that gift foremost in our mind each and every day we cross the threshold of our school's door. As we interact with colleagues and students, there is an inevitable confrontation over temporary and many times, insignificant issues. Keep the big picture in mind before entering into the conflict. How does it affect eternity? What will it matter even tomorrow? Pray in that split second of decision *(which will help us not to say something we will regret)* and seek to extend grace. It doesn't mean look the other way, it means to look right into the conflict and ask for His righteousness and grace to solve it in a way that will be pleasing to Him.

1:16 PM PRAYER

Please pray that our students and staff are safe at school.

QUOTE FOR THE DAY

You miss 100% of the shots you don't take. **Wayne Gretzky**

NOTES:

_____

_____

_____

_____

_____

DAY 48

#iamachristianeducator

Where we read the Bible with our brother and sisters in the public schools

DAILY PROMISES OF GOD
for educators

PSALM 119:36-38

NIV - *Turn my heart toward your statutes and not toward selfish gain. Turn my eyes away from worthless things; preserve my life according to your word. Fulfill your promise to your servant, so that you may be feared.*

RSV - *Incline my heart to thy testimonies, and not to gain! Turn my eyes from looking at vanities; and give me life in thy ways. Confirm to thy servant thy promise, which is for those who fear thee.*

KJV - *Incline my heart unto thy testimonies, and not to covetousness. Turn away mine eyes from beholding vanity; and quicken thou me in thy way. Stablish thy word unto thy servant, who is devoted to thy fear.*

LB - *Help me to prefer obedience to making money! Turn me away from wanting any other plan than yours. Revive my heart toward you. Reassure me that your promises are for me, for I trust and revere you.*

NOTE TO THE EDUCATOR

The Lord allows us to make our plans, but He directs our steps. What a generous God we serve. He affords us the ability to plan our ways, yet intercedes on our behalf by directing our ways. Let's take a look at our lesson plans. We are the ones who design our lessons, but what if we lifted each lesson up to Him before we planned it? It is a promise that He will direct our steps. Let's do it! Pray, plan and watch Him be the Director of our instruction.

1:16 PM PRAYER

Please pray that our Lord will be pleased with what we say, do and even think today.

QUOTE FOR THE DAY

If you only read the books that everyone else is reading, you can only think what everyone else is thinking. **Haruki Murakami, Norwegian Wood**

NOTES:
_____
_____
_____
_____
_____

Where we read the Bible with our brother and sisters in the public schools

DAILY PROMISES OF GOD
for educators

PSALM 119:41-42

DAY 50

NIV - *May your unfailing love come to me, Lord, your salvation, according to your promise; then I can answer anyone who taunts me, for I trust in your word.*

RSV - *Let thy steadfast love come to me, O Lord, thy salvation according to thy promise; then shall I have an answer for those who taunt me, for I trust in thy word.*

KJV - *Let thy mercies come also unto me, O Lord, even thy salvation, according to thy word. So shall I have wherewith to answer him that reproacheth me: for I trust in thy word.*

LB - *I long to obey them! Therefore in fairness renew my life, for this was your promise—yes, Lord, to save me! Now spare me by your kindness and your love. Then I will have an answer for those who taunt me, for I trust your promises.*

NOTE TO THE EDUCATOR

Being a Christian in the public schools is amazing. Did you realize that there are thousands of us, but we are not sure how or if we can interact? When you accepted the sacrifice of Jesus Christ as your Lord and Savior, you also allowed Him to remove all fear. He granted you salvation according to His promise. He has renewed you and has placed you on mission in the public schools of America that you may bless those with whom you interact with His Good News. If you have any questions/concerns about what you can and cannot do as a Christian in the public schools, do not hesitate to contact the servant leaders of CEAI (Christian Educators Association International) at www.ceai.org.

1:16 PM PRAYER

Please pray for any of our students who are sick.

QUOTE FOR THE DAY

The more that you read, the more things you will know. The more that you learn, the more places you'll go. **Dr. Seuss, I Can Read With My Eyes Shut!**

NOTES:

_____
_____
_____
_____
_____

#iamachristianeducator

Where we read the Bible with our brother and sisters in the public schools

DAILY PROMISES OF GOD
for educators

PSALM 119:49-50

NIV - *Remember your word to your servant, for you have given me hope. My comfort in my suffering is this: Your promise preserves my life.*

RSV - *Remember thy word to thy servant, in which thou hast made me hope. This is my comfort in my affliction that thy promise gives me life.*

KJV - *Remember the word unto thy servant, upon which thou hast caused me to hope. This is my comfort in my affliction: for thy word hath quickened me.*

LB - *Never forget your promises to me your servant, for they are my only hope. They give me strength in all my troubles; how they refresh and revive me!*

NOTE TO THE EDUCATOR

As we look into the promises of God this year, we frame everything thing around the hope that lies within us. For in Christ all the fullness of the Deity lives in bodily form (Col. 2:9) and He paid it all for us that we may live with Him eternally. That is our hope! That is His promise! He will never forget you. He will never leave you. Each day in school is another day closer to fully understanding His great gifts and living it out in our daily walk. Be refreshed today, dear Christian brother and sister in your position of dignity. Walk with Him through your daily routines and lessons. Look for ways to bless today because He has blessed us mightily.

1:16 PM PRAYER

Please pray that we may see our students as image bearers even when they do not act like it.

QUOTE FOR THE DAY

Make it simple, but significant. **Don Draper**

NOTES:

_____
_____
_____
_____
_____

Where we read the Bible with our brother and sisters in the public schools

DAILY PROMISES OF GOD
for educators

PSALM 119:57-58

DAY 52

NIV - *You are my portion, Lord; I have promised to obey your words. I have sought your face with all my heart; be gracious to me according to your promise.*

RSV - *The Lord is my portion; I promise to keep thy words. I entreat thy favor with all my heart; be gracious to me according to thy promise.*

KJV - *Thou art my portion, O Lord: I have said that I would keep thy words. I intreated thy favour with my whole heart: be merciful unto me according to thy word.*

LB - *Jehovah is mine! And I promise to obey! With all my heart I want your blessings. Be merciful just as you promised.*

NOTE TO THE EDUCATOR

Sometimes we think little things are not prayer worthy. Have you ever prayed to find lost items at school or for students who are sleeping in class? Every little thing that happens in our lives matters to God. It's unfathomable to us as human beings, but He is even concerned for the little sparrow! (Matt. 10:31) Seek His Face with all your heart. Call upon His wonderful ways, even for the small things. Also, be sensitive to the little needs of your students. They can't learn when they are upset about things that are important to them. Be like Jesus and be merciful to them because He has been merciful to us. Be gracious to your colleagues, because He has been gracious to us.

1:16 PM PRAYER

Please pray that we can encourage our students to be peacemakers.

QUOTE FOR THE DAY

Remember how far you've come, not just how far you have to go. You are not where you want to be, but neither are you where you used to be. **Rick Warren**

NOTES:
_____
_____
_____
_____
_____

#iamachristianeducator

 Where we read the Bible with our brother and sisters in the public schools

DAILY PROMISES OF GOD
for educators

PSALM 119:82

NIV - *My eyes fail, looking for your promise; I say, "When will you comfort me?"*

RSV - *My eyes fail with watching for thy promise; I ask, "When wilt thou comfort me?"*

KJV - *Mine eyes fail for thy word, saying, When wilt thou comfort me?*

LB - *My eyes are straining to see your promises come true. When will you comfort me with your help?*

NOTE TO THE EDUCATOR

You are not a bad Christian when you feel like He is not answering your prayers or when the school year is not going well. There will be a breakthrough, you can count on it. Why doesn't it happen the way we plan? While you are waiting for God to help you through the struggles this school year, rest assured that He is a covenant keeping God. Never stop praying for His wisdom, His guidance and His direction. As you become prayerfully dependent upon Him, He will give you direction, peace and mercy. If your year is going well, praise Him each day for the blessings and gifts. All good things come from Him.

1:16 PM PRAYER

Please pray for the student who feels isolated from his/her peers.

QUOTE FOR THE DAY

A candle loses nothing by lighting another candle. **James Keller**

NOTES:

_____
_____
_____
_____
_____

DAY 53

#iamachristianeducator

Where we read the Bible with our brother and sisters in the public schools

DAILY PROMISES OF GOD
for educators

PSALM 119:89

DAY 54

NIV - *Your word, Lord, is eternal; it stands firm in the heavens.*

RSV - *For ever, O Lord, thy word is firmly fixed in the heavens.*

KJV - *For ever, O Lord, thy word is settled in heaven.*

LB - *Forever, O Lord, your Word stands firm in heaven.*

NOTE TO THE EDUCATOR

The Word of God is living and active and sharper than any two-edged sword. (Hebrews 4:12). God's Word is eternal and why we long for it each day. I once heard a great quote, "*I have read many books, but the Bible is the only book that reads me.*" Being in the Word of God is the most essential tool for your success as an educator. It is our foundation as Christians and the manual of manuals. Make time for it, for it will richly bless your impact upon your students and colleagues. If you need to get up 15 minutes earlier, make it a new habit. Listen to the Word on Around the Word in 180 Days or Brian Hardin's Daily Audio Bible as you drive to school. Rely on the Word of God for it is your sword.

1:16 PM PRAYER

Please pray that we might show fellow educators and parents the grace the Lord has shown us.

QUOTE FOR THE DAY

There is a Book worth all other books which were ever printed. **Patrick Henry**

NOTES:

_____
_____
_____
_____
_____

#iamachristianeducator

Where we read the Bible with our brother and sisters in the public schools

DAILY PROMISES OF GOD
for educators

PSALM 119:105

DAY 55

NIV - *Your word is a lamp for my feet, a light on my path.*

RSV - *Thy word is a lamp to my feet and a light to my path.*

KJV - *Thy word is a lamp unto my feet, and a light unto my path.*

LB - *Your words are a flashlight to light the path ahead of me and keep me from stumbling.*

NOTE TO THE EDUCATOR

Sometimes the King James version is just so poetic – Thy Word is a lamp unto my feet, and a light unto my path. Commit this verse to memory so that you can pull it out in times of trouble or when you need a reminder that God is a promise keeping God. Listen to Amy Grant's version of this song and it will fill you with a peace that surpasses understanding. While you are walking the halls of your school, hum it to yourself and if you have the gift of meeting with a prayer group, share it with each other. There is great unity and hope in His Word as it breaks through all darkness and guides us in the way He would love for us to go. Don't forget that you are a light and a lamp for your students each and every day. They are always watching.

1:16 PM PRAYER

Please pray that we can see joy in adverse circumstances.

QUOTE FOR THE DAY

Life isn't about getting and having, it's about giving and being. **Kevin Kruse**

NOTES:
_____
_____
_____
_____
_____

#iamachristianeducator

Where we read the Bible with our brother and sisters in the public schools

DAILY PROMISES OF GOD
for educators

PSALM 119:116-117

DAY 56

NIV - *Sustain me, my God, according to your promise, and I will live; do not let my hopes be dashed. Uphold me, and I will be delivered; I will always have regard for your decrees.*

RSV - *Uphold me according to thy promise, that I may live, and let me not be put to shame in my hope! Hold me up, that I may be safe and have regard for thy statutes continually!*

KJV - *Uphold me according unto thy word, that I may live: and let me not be ashamed of my hope. Hold thou me up, and I shall be safe: and I will have respect unto thy statutes continually.*

LB - *Lord, you promised to let me live! Never let it be said that God failed me. Hold me safe above the heads of all my enemies; then I can continue to obey your laws.*

NOTE TO THE EDUCATOR

Do you think your students feel safe in your classroom? One of the main charges we have as educators is to create a safe learning environment for the children. In our times, safety is paramount. Creating a safe place for students in your classroom begins on your knees. It is the recognition that God is the One Who sustains us and holds us up. As we act as His agents in the field, one of our primary assignments is to keep His children safe. Do they feel loved? Do they feel comfortable to express themselves? Are they able to learn? All these questions are ongoing and require daily reflection. Lift these requests up to the ultimate Commander-in-Chief and Director of Security.

1:16 PM PRAYER

Please pray for our national and local elections. Pray for peace among all Americans.

QUOTE FOR THE DAY

This is the confidence that we have toward Him, that if we ask anything according to His will He hears us. **1 John 5:14**

NOTES:

_____
_____
_____
_____
_____

#iamachristianeducator

 Where we read the Bible with our brother and sisters in the public schools

DAILY PROMISES OF GOD
for educators

PSALM 119:148

NIV - *My eyes stay open through the watches of the night, that I may meditate on your promises.*

RSV - *My eyes are awake before the watches of the night, that I may meditate upon thy promise.*

KJV - *Mine eyes prevent the night watches, that I might meditate in thy word.*

LB - *I stay awake through the night to think about your promises.*

NOTE TO THE EDUCATOR

Meditation to a Christian is far different than a yoga position. When we meditate on God's Word we drink it in, we ask the Holy Spirit to teach us and show us the way. We read the Word to learn and to be inspired. The promises of God are a great way to slow down, ponder His greatness and mercy and ask Him for help. Many times we can be restless at night or just can't sleep. Turn the sleeplessness into an opportunity to meditate on His Word. If your mind is full of anxieties about tomorrow, meditate on His promises. He is faithful and steadfast, merciful and gracious to not only help you sleep, but to show you the way for tomorrow. Fear not, dear Christian educator, you serve a mighty God.

1:16 PM PRAYER

Please pray that the words of our mouth and the meditation of our hearts may be pleasing in God's sight. (Ps.19:14)

QUOTE FOR THE DAY

If you always put limits on everything you do, physical or anything else, it will spread into your work and into your life. There are no limits, only plateaus, and you must not stay there, you must go beyond them. **Bruce Lee**

NOTES:

_____
_____
_____
_____
_____

DAY 57

#iamachristianeducator

Where we read the Bible with our brother and sisters in the public schools

DAILY PROMISES OF GOD
for educators

PSALM 119:154

NIV - *Defend my cause and redeem me; preserve my life according to your promise.*

RSV - *Plead my cause and redeem me; give me life according to thy promise!*

KJV - *Plead my cause, and deliver me: quicken me according to thy word.*

LB - *Yes, rescue me and give me back my life again just as you have promised.*

NOTE TO THE EDUCATOR

By this time in the school year, we are settled, in theory. We know where we should be academically and where we need to go. We know our students well enough to know which ones need more tender-loving care. Did you realize that you can plead your cause before our Promise Keeper? Lift your curriculum timeline up to Him. Lift your struggling students up to Him and plead your causes before Him. Take the weight of the school year off your back and give it to Him. Once you have done that, the trick is not to take everything back. Trust Him to resolve the smallest and largest issues at your school.

1:16 PM PRAYER

Please pray for patience in today's stressful situations.

QUOTE FOR THE DAY

To look out at this kind of creation out here and not believe in God is to me impossible, ... It just strengthens my faith. I wish there were words to describe what it's like. **John Glenn**

NOTES:

_____
_____
_____
_____
_____

DAY 58

#iamachristianeducator

Where we read the Bible with our brother and sisters in the public schools

DAILY PROMISES OF GOD
for educators

PSALM 138:7

NIV - *Though I walk in the midst of trouble, you preserve my life. You stretch out your hand against the anger of my foes; with your right hand you save me.*

RSV - *Though I walk in the midst of trouble, thou dost preserve my life; thou dost stretch out thy hand against the wrath of my enemies, and thy right hand delivers me.*

KJV - *Though I walk in the midst of trouble, thou wilt revive me: thou shalt stretch forth thine hand against the wrath of mine enemies, and thy right hand shall save me.*

LB - *Though I am surrounded by troubles, you will bring me safely through them. You will clench your fist against my angry enemies! Your power will save me.*

NOTE TO THE EDUCATOR

How are the first year teachers doing on your campus? Have you checked in on them lately? Are you a new teacher? This is the hardest year in teaching because NO ONE can take in all the variables of maintaining a classroom. We are covered in the midst of troubles. We are revived by His presence. If you are a veteran teacher, check on one of the newest teachers to your staff. Give them this verse as an encouragement. If you are one of the newbies, praise God for His saving promises. Don't be afraid to admit that you need help. He is ever ready and so are the Christian educators on your campus.

1:16 PM PRAYER

Please pray that we do our best according to Col. 3:17.

QUOTE FOR THE DAY

Find joy in the ordinary. **Unknown**

NOTES:
_____
_____
_____
_____
_____

DAY 59

#iamachristianeducator

Where we read the Bible with our brother and sisters in the public schools

DAILY PROMISES OF GOD
for educators

PSALM 139:13-16

NIV - *For you created my inmost being; you knit me together in my mother's womb. I praise you because I am fearfully and wonderfully made; your works are wonderful, I know that full well. My frame was not hidden from you when I was made in the secret place, when I was woven together in the depths of the earth. Your eyes saw my unformed body; all the days ordained for me were written in your book before one of them came to be.*

RSV - *For thou didst form my inward parts, thou didst knit me together in my mother's womb. I praise thee, for thou art fearful and wonderful. Wonderful are thy works. Thou knowest me right well; my frame was not hidden from thee, when I was being made in secret, intricately wrought in the depths of the earth. Thy eyes beheld my unformed substance; in thy book were written, every one of them, the days that were formed for me, when as yet there was none of them.*

KJV - *For thou hast possessed my reins: thou hast covered me in my mother's womb. I will praise thee; for I am fearfully and wonderfully made: marvellous are thy works; and that my soul knoweth right well. My substance was not hid from thee, when I was made in secret, and curiously wrought in the lowest parts of the earth. Thine eyes did see my substance, yet being unperfect; and in thy book all my members were written, which in continuance were fashioned, when as yet there was none of them.*

LB - *You made all the delicate, inner parts of my body and knit them together in my mother's womb. Thank you for making me so wonderfully complex! It is amazing to think about. Your workmanship is marvelous—and how well I know it. You were there while I was being formed in utter seclusion! You saw me before I was born and scheduled each day of my life before I began to breathe. Every day was recorded in your book!*

NOTE TO THE EDUCATOR

We are in the Book! We are intricately woven. We are His children. What a precious promise to know where we have come from and where we are going. All the days of our lives are ordained. You are not an educator by chance. You have been ordained. Stand strong, Christian educator and praise Him for His marvelous deeds.

1:16 PM PRAYER

Please pray for the families in our school communities who are having trouble paying for their utilities.

QUOTE FOR THE DAY

Confidence is quiet. Insecurity is loud. **Unknown**

NOTES:

_____

_____

_____

_____

DAY 60

#iamachristianeducator

Where we read the Bible with our brother and sisters in the public schools

DAILY PROMISES OF GOD
for educators

PSALM 145:13

NIV - *Your kingdom is an everlasting kingdom, and your dominion endures through all generations. The Lord is trustworthy in all he promises and faithful in all he does.*

RSV - *Thy kingdom is an everlasting kingdom, and thy dominion endures throughout all generations. The Lord is faithful in all his words, and gracious in all his deeds.*

KJV - *Thy kingdom is an everlasting kingdom, and thy dominion endureth throughout all generations.*

LB - *For your kingdom never ends. You rule generation after generation.*

NOTE TO THE EDUCATOR

Let us pray.
Dear Father,
Thank You Lord for Your dominion that endures for generations. Thank You for allowing us to touch the generations for You. Show us Lord how to be Your ambassadors Your way. Teach us, O Lord to be in awe of Your everlasting kingdom and place in perspective our issues at school as they compare to Your eternal promises for us. Lord, thank You for Your beauty, Your grace, Your mercy, Your compassion and love. Help us to be like You each and every day, each and every minute at school. We love You, Lord and ask this in the mighty Name of Jesus, Amen.

1:16 PM PRAYER

Please pray that we may have balance at home and at school as well.

QUOTE FOR THE DAY

Whatever the mind of man can conceive and believe, it can achieve. **Napoleon Hill**

NOTES:

_____
_____
_____
_____
_____

Where we read the Bible with our brother and sisters in the public schools

DAILY PROMISES OF GOD
for educators

PSALM 145:16

DAY 62

NIV - *You open your hand and satisfy the desires of every living thing.*

RSV - *Thou openest thy hand, thou satisfiest the desire of every living thing.*

KJV - *Thou openest thine hand, and satisfiest the desire of every living thing.*

LB - *You constantly satisfy the hunger and thirst of every living thing.*

NOTE TO THE EDUCATOR

The greatest desires of mankind can only be satisfied by God Himself. He has created us with a God-sized hole in our hearts that can be filled with so many things, but nothing satisfies us as well as God. His consistency and unfailing love is amazing. Let us thank Him every day. Our students come to school each day with unsatisfied desires. We have no way of satisfying their needs as God will, but we can be mindful of a safe environment where they can grow, gain knowledge, express themselves and love to learn. We can give them our whole heart, mind and soul in everything we do. They know the difference between wholehearted commitments and half-hearted ones. Let's be wholly devoted to their well-being in our school environments.

1:16 PM PRAYER

Please pray that students will have the courage to be honest.

QUOTE FOR THE DAY

Life is what happens to you while you're busy making other plans. **John Lennon**

NOTES:
_____
_____
_____
_____
_____

Where we read the Bible with our brother and sisters in the public schools

#iamachristianeducator

DAILY PROMISES OF GOD
for educators

PSALM 146:5-8

NIV - *Blessed are those whose help is the God of Jacob, whose hope is in the Lord their God. He is the Maker of heaven and earth, the sea, and everything in them—he remains faithful forever. He upholds the cause of the oppressed and gives food to the hungry. The Lord sets prisoners free, the Lord gives sight to the blind, the Lord lifts up those who are bowed down, the Lord loves the righteous.*

RSV - *Happy is he whose help is the God of Jacob, whose hope is in the Lord his God, who made heaven and earth, the sea, and all that is in them; who keeps faith for ever; who executes justice for the oppressed; who gives food to the hungry. The Lord sets the prisoners free; the Lord opens the eyes of the blind. The Lord lifts up those who are bowed down; the Lord loves the righteous.*

KJV - *Happy is he that hath the God of Jacob for his help, whose hope is in the Lord his God: Which made heaven, and earth, the sea, and all that therein is: which keepeth truth for ever: Which executeth judgment for the oppressed: which giveth food to the hungry. The Lord looseth the prisoners: The Lord openeth the eyes of the blind: the Lord raiseth them that are bowed down: the Lord loveth the righteous.*

LB - *But happy is the man who has the God of Jacob as his helper, whose hope is in the Lord his God— the God who made both earth and heaven, the seas and everything in them. He is the God who keeps every promise, who gives justice to the poor and oppressed and food to the hungry. He frees the prisoners and opens the eyes of the blind; he lifts the burdens from those bent down beneath their loads. For the Lord loves good men.*

NOTE TO THE EDUCATOR

Our public schools are the largest mission field in the nation. Among us are the oppressed, the hungry, the imprisoned, the blind and those who are bowed down. We serve His people by doing what He would do. I don't know how many times I have seen students misbehave or score poorly on tests, or refuse to do assignments when the underlying reason was hunger. When one of your students is struggling next time, ask them if they are hungry. Store some granola bars or non-perishable healthy foods and privately feed them. It may be one of the greatest acts of kindness a child needs. We know that is what Jesus would do.

1:16 PM PRAYER

Please pray to we remember that we are all God's children.

QUOTE FOR THE DAY

Every child is an artist. The problem is how to remain an artist once he grows up. **Pablo Picasso**

NOTES:

_____

_____

_____

_____

 Where we read the Bible with our brother and sisters in the public schools

DAY 63

#iamachristianeducator

DAILY PROMISES OF GOD
for educators

PSALM 146:9

NIV - *The Lord watches over the foreigner and sustains the fatherless and the widow, but he frustrates the ways of the wicked.*

RSV - *The Lord watches over the sojourners, he upholds the widow and the fatherless; but the way of the wicked he brings to ruin.*

KJV - *The Lord preserveth the strangers; he relieveth the fatherless and widow: but the way of the wicked he turneth upside down.*

LB - *He protects the immigrants and cares for the orphans and widows. But he turns topsy-turvy the plans of the wicked.*

NOTE TO THE EDUCATOR

Depending on where you are in the United States of America, immigrant children are a major part of the public school community. Many of these children have unique disadvantages: language barriers, cultural differences, lack of parental support on school assignments/projects and are more subject to ridicule and bullying. As His people, we can set a keen eye on their difficulties. We can offer assistance and praise. We can show them unconditional love. We can pray for them and ask God to fulfill His promise to them. He is the One Who watches over the sojourners, the foreigners, the strangers and the immigrants. Let us rejoice in Him.

1:16 PM PRAYER

Please pray that the words we speak are a purposeful blessing today.

QUOTE FOR THE DAY

I've learned that people will forget what you said, people will forget what you did, but people will never forget how you made them feel. **Maya Angelou**

NOTES:

_____
_____
_____
_____
_____

Where we read the Bible with our brother and sisters in the public schools

DAILY PROMISES OF GOD
for educators

PSALM 147:3

NIV - *He heals the brokenhearted and binds up their wounds.*

RSV - *He heals the brokenhearted, and binds up their wounds.*

KJV - *He healeth the broken in heart, and bindeth up their wounds.*

LB - *He heals the brokenhearted, binding up their wounds.*

NOTE TO THE EDUCATOR

In every school where I have taught, there is a Sunshine Committee whose sole responsibility is to send flowers, cards and condolences to staff members who have lost loved ones or have great troubles. We each chip in a small amount of money and then the needs of the grieving or troubled are met in a small way. As Christian educators, we are the SONshine Committee. Christ followers are comforted by His power to bind our wounds, but what happens to those that don't believe? I don't know how anyone can go through hard times without Him. We can step up with prayers, cards, acknowledgments that we want to serve them and check in on them when all the cards and calls slow down. We can be His agents of mercy during these very difficult times of heartbreak. These difficult times are a great opportunity to show Jesus to our hurting colleagues.

1:16 PM PRAYER

Please pray for a lifting of the heavy burdens our teachers are feeling.

QUOTE FOR THE DAY

All Scripture is God-breathed and He doesn't waste His breath. **Jim Cotter**

NOTES:
_____
_____
_____
_____
_____

Where we read the Bible with our brother and sisters in the public schools

DAILY PROMISES OF GOD
for educators

PROVERBS 1:33

NIV - *But whoever listens to me will live in safety and be at ease, without fear of harm.*

RSV - *But he who listens to me will dwell secure and will be at ease, without dread of evil.*

KJV - *But whoso hearkeneth unto me shall dwell safely, and shall be quiet from fear of evil.*

LB - *But all who listen to me shall live in peace and safety, unafraid.*

NOTE TO THE EDUCATOR

God is not promising there will never be fear, evil or harm in our lives or the lives of our students, but He does comfort us with the reminder that He is the Ultimate Director of Security. He alone can bring us through tragedy. We are not to fear or dwell on all the evil things that might happen. Instead, we need to be diligent, well-trained in how to protect our students from harm and then place the safety and peace of our campus in His Hands. When we dwell in safety and are quiet from the fear of evil, a whole lot more learning can go on. Praise God for His watch over us. Fear not, Christian brothers and sisters.

1:16 PM PRAYER

Please pray for any student or colleague who is suffering from anxiety.

QUOTE FOR THE DAY

I would rather belong to a poor nation that was free than to a rich nation that had ceased to be in love with liberty. **Woodrow Wilson**

NOTES:

_____
_____
_____
_____
_____

DAY 66

#iamachristianeducator

 Where we read the Bible with our brother and sisters in the public schools

DAILY PROMISES OF GOD
for educators

PROVERBS 3:3-4

NIV - *Let love and faithfulness never leave you; bind them around your neck, write them on the tablet of your heart. Then you will win favor and a good name in the sight of God and man. Trust in the Lord with all your heart and lean not on your own understanding;*

RSV - *Let not loyalty and faithfulness forsake you; bind them about your neck, write them on the tablet of your heart. So you will find favor and good repute in the sight of God and man. Trust in the Lord with all your heart, and do not rely on your own insight.*

KJV - *Let not mercy and truth forsake thee: bind them about thy neck; write them upon the table of thine heart: So shalt thou find favour and good understanding in the sight of God and man. Trust in the Lord with all thine heart; and lean not unto thine own understanding.*

LB - *Never tire of loyalty and kindness. Hold these virtues tightly. Write them deep within your heart. If you want favor with both God and man, and a reputation for good judgment and common sense, then trust the Lord completely; don't ever trust yourself.*

NOTE TO THE EDUCATOR

One of the admonitions I have given my daughters is to be a "learn-it-all", not a "know-it-all." God's powerful Word is living and active and will give us the knowledge and wisdom for every human situation we might find in our schools. Trust Him for the answer to your questions. Trust Him for the instructional method and style that He created in You. Ask Him for help each and every day before You begin your day or even before each lesson you teach. Be faithful to your school and always, always, always do that right thing before the Lord. Then you will even have favor with your students and colleagues. May it all point to Him and give Him the glory.

1:16 PM PRAYER

Please pray for a prayer partner and fellowship on your campus.

QUOTE FOR THE DAY

When one side only of a story is heard and often repeated, the human mind becomes impressed with it insensibly. **George Washington**

NOTES:

_____

_____

_____

_____

_____

Where we read the Bible with our brother and sisters in the public schools

DAILY PROMISES OF GOD
for educators

PROVERBS 3:11-12

NIV - *My son, do not despise the Lord's discipline, and do not resent his rebuke because the Lord disciplines those he loves, as a father the son he delights in.*

RSV - *My son, do not despise the Lord's discipline or be weary of his reproof, for the Lord reproves him whom he loves, as a father the son in whom he delights.*

KJV - *My son, despise not the chastening of the Lord; neither be weary of his correction: For whom the Lord loveth he correcteth; even as a father the son in whom he delighteth.*

LB - *Young man, do not resent it when God chastens and corrects you, for his punishment is proof of his love. Just as a father punishes a son he delights in to make him better, so the Lord corrects you.*

NOTE TO THE EDUCATOR

Discipline is the proof of God's love. What a bold statement. Christians understand that God is faithful to correct us when we are wrong. He has promised to guide us, lead us and help us change course when we are on the wrong path. As Christian educators, we have the charge to discipline our students in love. Many times it is easier to turn a blind eye to a misbehavior, but what if God did that? God loves us so much that He is willing to correct us to make us better, to mold us into all that we can be. We need to look at each of our students and correct them in order to help them grow and reach their God-given potential. Letting them settle for less is not acceptable.

1:16 PM PRAYER

Please pray for His presence to be evident in us today.

QUOTE FOR THE DAY

Think about every problem, every challenge, we face. The solution to each starts with education. **George H.W. Bush**

NOTES:

_____
_____
_____
_____
_____

 Where we read the Bible with our brother and sisters in the public schools

DAILY PROMISES OF GOD
for educators

PROVERBS 14:27

NIV - *The fear of the Lord is a fountain of life, turning a person from the snares of death.*

RSV - *The fear of the Lord is a fountain of life, that one may avoid the snares of death.*

KJV - *The fear of the Lord is a fountain of life, to depart from the snares of death.*

LB - *Reverence for the Lord is a fountain of life; its waters keep a man from death.*

NOTE TO THE EDUCATOR

The Lord is a fountain of life. Learning to be prayerfully dependent upon Him helps us to avoid unnecessary falter in the classroom. Can you imagine what your classroom would be like if it were a fountain of life? Things would flourish, be refreshed and renewed. Purposely covering our classrooms, hallways, gymnasiums, cafeterias and auditoriums with the fruit of the Spirit as given by the Lord is the fountain of life for education. How can that possibly be done? By our power, it is impossible, but through Christ alone all things are possible. Ask a prayer partner to begin prayer walking your campus. Target specific areas that need the most life breathed into them. Make a circuit around your campus and over time you will be able to cover your school. Prayer walking continually is a commitment well worth the effort.

1:16 PM PRAYER

Please pray for diligence in planning and preparation.

QUOTE FOR THE DAY

A president's hardest task is not to do what is right, but to know what is right. **Lyndon Johnson**

NOTES:

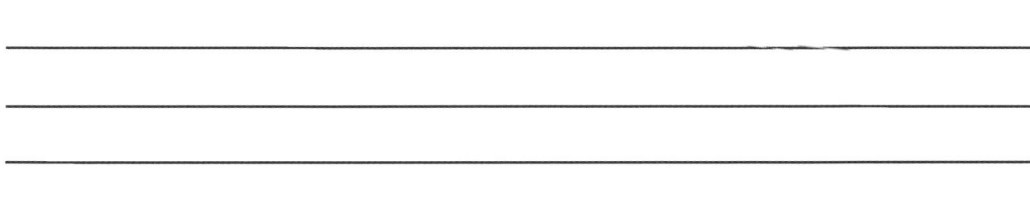

_____
_____
_____
_____
_____

Where we read the Bible with our brother and sisters in the public schools

DAILY PROMISES OF GOD
for educators

PROVERBS 16:3

NIV - *Commit to the Lord whatever you do, and he will establish your plans.*

RSV - *Commit your work to the Lord, and your plans will be established.*

KJV - *Commit thy works unto the Lord, and thy thoughts shall be established.*

LB - *Commit your work to the Lord, then it will succeed.*

NOTE TO THE EDUCATOR

Have you dedicated your classroom to the Lord? Have you dedicated your campus to the Lord? He owns it all. He owns the cattle on a thousand hills. He owns your school. If you have not committed your classroom to Him, consider it. When I took the Crown Ministries course for finances, they had us write out a deed and sign over all our money and possessions back to the Lord. Let's do the same for our schools. Create a deed that proclaims God as the owner of the school. Relinquish all rights of ownership to Him. Accept all responsibilities of being a good steward of His properties, His children and His gifts. Create the deed on paper, sign it and then hang it in your personal spot within your classroom or office as a daily reminder. Commit it all to Him and He will establish your success. It's a promise.

1:16 PM PRAYER

Please pray that our students honor their parents.

QUOTE FOR THE DAY

The consequences arising from the continual accumulation of public debts in other countries ought to admonish us to be careful to prevent their growth in our own. **John Adams**

NOTES:
_____
_____
_____
_____
_____
_____

Where we read the Bible with our brother and sisters in the public schools

DAILY PROMISES OF GOD
for educators

PROVERBS 18:10

NIV - *The name of the Lord is a fortified tower; the righteous run to it and are safe.*

RSV - *The name of the Lord is a strong tower; the righteous man runs into it and is safe.*

KJV - *The name of the Lord is a strong tower: the righteous runneth into it, and is safe.*

LB - *The Lord is a strong fortress. The godly run to him and are safe.*

NOTE TO THE EDUCATOR

If you are a listener to Around the Word in 180 Days, you know that I open the podcast with an ABC prayer of adoration. He taught us to pray in the pattern of the Lord's prayer and the first part is "Hallowed be Thy Name." God's Name is our refuge and strength, our high tower. It is comfort and is safe. Knowing multiple names and attributes of God enhances our love for Him. The next time you pray with your brothers and sisters in the public school, open the prayer time by going around the room and having each person speak a name/attribute of God in ABC order. It may go something like this: Abba, Bread of Life, Comforter, Designer, Extraordinary, Father, Gracious, Holy, Incredible, Jesus, King of Kings, Lord of Lords, Messiah, Name Above all Names, Omnipotent, Powerful, Quieter of our Souls, Rescuer, Sustainer, Teacher of Teachers, Unmatched, Victorious, Wonderful, eXpert, Yahweh, Zenith overall. Let us run to Him, the only place we will always be safe in our public schools.

1:16 PM PRAYER

Please pray for the courage to stand up for that which honors the Lord.

QUOTE FOR THE DAY

The more that you read, the more things you will know. The more that you learn, the more places you'll go. **Dr. Seuss, I Can Read With My Eyes Shut!**

NOTES:
_____
_____
_____
_____
_____

DAY 71

#iamachristianeducator

 *Where we read the Bible with our brother and sisters in the public schools*

DAILY PROMISES OF GOD
for educators

PROVERBS 19:17

NIV - *Whoever is kind to the poor lends to the Lord, and he will reward them for what they have done.*

RSV - *He who is kind to the poor lends to the Lord, and he will repay him for his deed.*

KJV - *He that hath pity upon the poor lendeth unto the Lord; and that which he hath given will he pay him again.*

LB - *When you help the poor you are lending to the Lord—and he pays wonderful interest on your loan!*

NOTE TO THE EDUCATOR

Working with our poorest students is lending to the Lord! I love how the Living Bible translates the second half of the verse – and He pays wonderful interest on your loan! I've never thought about working with our poor students as a loan, but the Lord loves children and is the Champion of the poor. He told us in Matt. 26:11 that we will always have the poor with us and He always admonishes us to take care of the poor. How can we do that at school? Make a special effort to know the backgrounds of the students who are struggling financially. Seek ways to tutor the most disadvantage. Education is one of the greatest gifts we can give the poor that they may help themselves. Never underestimate your impact on the poorest of your students.

1:16 PM PRAYER

Please pray that our students will be kind to one another.

QUOTE FOR THE DAY

Be yourself; everyone else is already taken. **Oscar Wilde**

NOTES:

_____
_____
_____
_____
_____

DAY 72

#iamachristianeducator

Where we read the Bible with our brother and sisters in the public schools

DAILY PROMISES OF GOD
for educators

PROVERBS 19:21

NIV - *Many are the plans in a person's heart, but it is the Lord's purpose that prevails.*

RSV - *Many are the plans in the mind of a man, but it is the purpose of the Lord that will be established.*

KJV - *There are many devices in a man's heart; nevertheless the counsel of the Lord, that shall stand.*

LB - *There are many plans in a man's heart, but it is the Lord's plan that will stand.*

NOTE TO THE EDUCATOR

Dear Christian educator,

You may think you became an educator because of your hard work. It is partially true. However, our gracious God sowed into you the gift of teaching. Your heart burned to become an educator because it is His purpose. Being a purpose-driven educator is such a gift to your school because you will only do those things that are right and just for your students. Will you make mistakes? Of course, but you will repent and change and look to the Only One Who can forgive. You may have planned to be an educator, but it is the Lord's purpose for you to excel. Thank Him today for this great gift and high calling.

1:16 PM PRAYER

Please pray that we remember to give thanks to our Creator for all He has done for us.

QUOTE FOR THE DAY

Problems are not stop signs, they are guidelines. **Mark Twain**

NOTES:
_____
_____
_____
_____
_____

DAY 73

#iamachristianeducator

Where we read the Bible with our brother and sisters in the public schools

DAILY PROMISES OF GOD
for educators

ISAIAH 11:9

DAY 74

NIV - *They will neither harm nor destroy on all my holy mountain, for the earth will be filled with the knowledge of the Lord as the waters cover the sea.*

RSV - *They shall not hurt or destroy in all my holy mountain; for the earth shall be full of the knowledge of the Lord as the waters cover the sea.*

KJV - *They shall not hurt nor destroy in all my holy mountain: for the earth shall be full of the knowledge of the Lord, as the waters cover the sea.*

LB - *Nothing will hurt or destroy in all my holy mountain, for as the waters fill the sea, so shall the earth be full of the knowledge of the Lord.*

NOTE TO THE EDUCATOR

If you haven't downloaded or checked out the Promise Cards that match this companion, please feel free to get them in our app, Facebook page or www.aw180days.com and share. Each card has the promise for the school day overlaid on a sunrise picture that I took at the water's edge. It is this verse (Isa. 11:9) that proclaims our future and hope when the knowledge of the Lord will cover the earth as the waters cover the sea. We live in the right now, but we fully understand that there will come a time when every head will bow, every knee will bend and every tongue will confess that Jesus is Lord. Each time we see a new sunrise, it is the reminder of His great faithfulness through new mercies each day (Lam. 3:23) and His promise when everyone will know Him!

1:16 PM PRAYER

Please pray for kindness and gentleness in our speech.

QUOTE FOR THE DAY

The rights of man come not from the generosity of the state but from the hand of God. **John F. Kennedy**

NOTES:

_____
_____
_____
_____
_____

#iamachristianeducator

Where we read the Bible with our brother and sisters in the public schools

DAILY PROMISES OF GOD
for educators

ISAIAH 12:2

NIV - *Surely God is my salvation; I will trust and not be afraid. The Lord, the Lord himself, is my strength and my defense; he has become my salvation.*

RSV - *Behold, God is my salvation; I will trust, and will not be afraid; for the Lord God is my strength and my song, and he has become my salvation.*

KJV - *Behold, God is my salvation; I will trust, and not be afraid: for the Lord Jehovah is my strength and my song; he also is become my salvation.*

LB - *See, God has come to save me! I will trust and not be afraid, for the Lord is my strength and song; he is my salvation.*

NOTE TO THE EDUCATOR

How is your week going? They say that Tuesday is the most productive day. Monday, the students are dragging in after the weekend. Wednesday, they are half-way there. Thursday, they are already looking toward the weekend and Friday – well forget about it. Tuesday is best to raise the bar and their productivity. It applies to us too. Why not claim one day of the week to be the day we all pray with a least one other colleague. He is our salvation. We share that hope. He is our strength and defense. We share that gift. We cannot be afraid. You can legally and gracefully pray with a colleague as long as it is before or after your contract time. Let's commit to giving Him one day each week to partner in a prayer of thanksgiving.

1:16 PM PRAYER

Please pray for the self-control that comes only from the Holy Spirit.

QUOTE FOR THE DAY

Don't watch the clock; do what it does. Keep going. **Ayn Rand**

NOTES:

_____

_____

_____

_____

_____

Where we read the Bible with our brother and sisters in the public schools

DAILY PROMISES OF GOD
for educators

ISAIAH 40:29-31

NIV - *He gives strength to the weary and increases the power of the weak. Even youths grow tired and weary, and young men stumble and fall; but those who hope in the Lord will renew their strength. They will soar on wings like eagles; they will run and not grow weary, they will walk and not be faint.*

RSV - *He gives power to the faint, and to him who has no might he increases strength. Even youths shall faint and be weary, and young men shall fall exhausted; but they who wait for the Lord shall renew their strength, they shall mount up with wings like eagles, they shall run and not be weary, they shall walk and not faint.*

KJV - *He giveth power to the faint; and to them that have no might he increaseth strength. Even the youths shall faint and be weary, and the young men shall utterly fall: But they that wait upon the Lord shall renew their strength; they shall mount up with wings as eagles; they shall run, and not be weary; and they shall walk, and not faint.*

LB - *He gives power to the tired and worn out, and strength to the weak. Even the youths shall be exhausted, and the young men will all give up. But they that wait upon the Lord shall renew their strength. They shall mount up with wings like eagles; they shall run and not be weary; they shall walk and not faint.*

NOTE TO THE EDUCATOR

Weary is a perfect adjective for school life. Students get weary. Teachers get weary. Support staff, substitutes, administrators and parents get weary. When you feel weary, rest in this promise. When you wait upon the Lord, He always over delivers. What a beautiful picture of flying high like an eagle over the burdens of our days.

Dear Lord,
   Thank You for this incredible promise that anchors us in You when we are weary. Help us to not succumb to weariness, but to look to You for renewal. We love you, Lord. Amen.

1:16 PM PRAYER

Please pray for any student or colleague who is struggling with depression.

QUOTE FOR THE DAY

What you do today can improve all your tomorrows. **Sam Levenson**

NOTES:

_____
_____
_____
_____
_____

DAY 76

#iamachristianeducator

 Where we read the Bible with our brother and sisters in the public schools

DAILY PROMISES OF GOD
for educators
ISAIAH 41:10

NIV - *So do not fear, for I am with you; do not be dismayed, for I am your God.
I will strengthen you and help you; I will uphold you with my righteous right hand.*

RSV - *Fear not, for I am with you, be not dismayed, for I am your God; I will strengthen you,
I will help you, I will uphold you with my victorious right hand.*

KJV - *Fear thou not; for I am with thee: be not dismayed; for I am thy God: I will strengthen
thee; yea, I will help thee; yea, I will uphold thee with the right hand of my righteousness.*

LB - *Fear not, for I am with you. Do not be dismayed. I am your God. I will strengthen you;
I will help you; I will uphold you with my victorious right hand.*

NOTE TO THE EDUCATOR

Victory comes from the Lord. Do you have a difficult student that is always on your mind? Victory over this trial comes from the Lord. Pray for that student. Ask God to give the student victory over their issues. Ask the student how you can serve them. For secondary students, that question may come as a shock. They may not have ever had an adult ask how they can serve them. For elementary students, they may not know what you mean, but they will know that you are not yelling at them! Ask the Lord for strength and wisdom to be a servant to the difficult students. They definitely have the power to make or break your year. Why allow it to escalate? Pray for victory over the issue because we serve a God with a victorious right hand.

1:16 PM PRAYER

Please pray that we create prayer groups at school which offer a place of grace and peace.

QUOTE FOR THE DAY

Keep your eyes on the stars, and your feet on the ground. **Walt Disney**

NOTES:
_____
_____
_____
_____
_____

DAY 77

#iamachristianeducator

Where we read the Bible with our brother and sisters in the public schools

DAILY PROMISES OF GOD
for educators

ISAIAH 43:1-2

NIV - *But now, this is what the Lord says— he who created you, Jacob, he who formed you, Israel: "Do not fear, for I have redeemed you; I have summoned you by name; you are mine. When you pass through the waters, I will be with you; and when you pass through the rivers, they will not sweep over you. When you walk through the fire, you will not be burned; the flames will not set you ablaze.*

RSV - *But now thus says the Lord, he who created you, O Jacob, he who formed you, O Israel: "Fear not, for I have redeemed you; I have called you by name, you are mine. When you pass through the waters I will be with you; and through the rivers, they shall not overwhelm you; when you walk through fire you shall not be burned, and the flame shall not consume you.*

KJV - *But now thus saith the Lord that created thee, O Jacob, and he that formed thee, O Israel, Fear not: for I have redeemed thee, I have called thee by thy name; thou art mine. When thou passest through the waters, I will be with thee; and through the rivers, they shall not overflow thee: when thou walkest through the fire, thou shalt not be burned; neither shall the flame kindle upon thee.*

LB - *But now the Lord who created you, O Israel, says: Don't be afraid, for I have ransomed you; I have called you by name; you are mine. When you go through deep waters and great trouble, I will be with you. When you go through rivers of difficulty, you will not drown! When you walk through the fire of oppression, you will not be burned up—the flames will not consume you.*

NOTE TO THE EDUCATOR

The Lord has promised Israel and Jacob great things. How much more has He promised to those of us who are grafted in through Jesus Christ? Brothers and sisters, we stand together against all the powers and authorities that are enemies of God. We stand together to be ambassadors and light to the dark places in our public schools. We stand together knowing that the rivers of pressures from the district and state cannot overwhelm us. We stand together through the fire of attack on our profession. Since when has the teacher become the bad guy? We stand together as Christian educators with the solid foundation of Christ alone.

1:16 PM PRAYER

Please pray for the needs of the cafeteria workers on your campus.

QUOTE FOR THE DAY

Your talent is God's gift to you. What you do with it is your gift back to God. **C.S. Lewis**

NOTES:

_____

_____

_____

_____

DAY 78

#iamachristianeducator

Where we read the Bible with our brother and sisters in the public schools

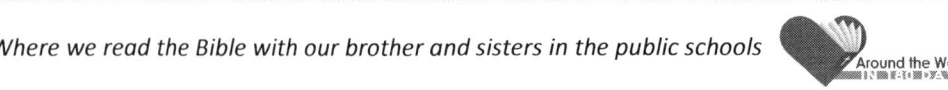

DAILY PROMISES OF GOD
for educators

ISAIAH 44:22

NIV - *I have swept away your offenses like a cloud, your sins like the morning mist. Return to me, for I have redeemed you.*

RSV - *I have swept away your transgressions like a cloud, and your sins like mist return to me, for I have redeemed you.*

KJV - *I have blotted out, as a thick cloud, thy transgressions, and, as a cloud, thy sins: return unto me; for I have redeemed thee.*

LB - *I've blotted out your sins; they are gone like morning mist at noon! Oh, return to me, for I have paid the price to set you free.*

NOTE TO THE EDUCATOR

Perhaps you feel estranged from God at times. You mean to pray in the morning, but the kids got up earlier than usual, or your alarm didn't go off. There's no guilt. Perhaps you mean to read the Bible more, but papers are piling up, to-do lists are lengthening and you see no end in sight. There is no guilt. All God asks is that you return to Him. He has you covered. He doesn't want you to worry about your burdens. He has taken away all your sins like the morning mist at noon! (love that line) Return to Him. He is calling you. Pray right now. Read these verses right now and return to Him. He has set you free from all burdens and sins.

1:16 PM PRAYER

Please pray for the ability to pray discretely and reverently at 1:16PM each school day.

QUOTE FOR THE DAY

Life is really simple, but we insist on making in complicated. **Aldous Huxley**

NOTES:
_____
_____
_____
_____
_____

DAY 79

#iamachristianeducator

Where we read the Bible with our brother and sisters in the public schools

DAILY PROMISES OF GOD
for educators

ISAIAH 46:4

NIV - *Even to your old age and gray hairs I am he, I am he who will sustain you. I have made you and I will carry you; I will sustain you and I will rescue you.*

RSV - *Even to your old age I am He, and to gray hairs I will carry you. I have made, and I will bear; I will carry and will save.*

KJV - *And even to your old age I am he; and even to hoar hairs will I carry you: I have made, and I will bear; even I will carry, and will deliver you.*

LB - *I will be your God through all your lifetime, yes, even when your hair is white with age. I made you and I will care for you. I will carry you along and be your Savior.*

NOTE TO THE EDUCATOR

Who is this loving God we serve? He is even reminding us that He loves us for a lifetime. Whether we are a first year educator or one about to retire with gray hair, He is the One Who sustains us. When we are young, we can't imagine being old, but getting old has great benefits. We have a lifelong God. We strive to instill lifelong learning in our students, but what about lifelong loving? We love God because He loves us first, but have we made a lifelong commitment to that love as He has? Dearest brothers and sisters, let us pray today for the strength, faith, belief and power of the Holy Spirit to love our Lord with a lifelong love.

1:16 PM PRAYER

Please pray to be Jesus with skin on to all those you interact with today.

QUOTE FOR THE DAY

England has two books; the Bible and Shakespeare. England made Shakespeare, but the Bible made England. **Victor Hugo**

NOTES:

_____
_____
_____
_____
_____

DAY 80

#iamachristianeducator

Where we read the Bible with our brother and sisters in the public schools

DAILY PROMISES OF GOD
for educators
ISAIAH 46:9-10

NIV - *Remember the former things, those of long ago; I am God, and there is no other; I am God, and there is none like me. I make known the end from the beginning, from ancient times, what is still to come. I say, 'My purpose will stand, and I will do all that I please.*

RSV - *Remember the former things of old; for I am God, and there is no other; I am God, and there is none like me, declaring the end from the beginning and from ancient times things not yet done, saying, 'My counsel shall stand, and I will accomplish all my purpose,*

KJV - *Remember the former things of old: for I am God, and there is none else; I am God, and there is none like me, Declaring the end from the beginning, and from ancient times the things that are not yet done, saying, My counsel shall stand, and I will do all my pleasure.*

LB - *And don't forget the many times I clearly told you what was going to happen in the future. For I am God—I only—and there is no other like me who can tell you what is going to happen. All I say will come to pass, for I do whatever I wish.*

NOTE TO THE EDUCATOR

Hindsight is 20-20. Only God can see the past, present and future. He declares the end from the beginning. How does He do that? He is God and there is no other. Rather than trying to figure out how He works, let's bask in His pleasure to do whatever He wishes. Thankfully for us, His is only concerned for our good, our well-being and success. If you are not sure how you will succeed this school year, try to look back on the times He has pulled you through. At the time, it always feels impossible, but in hindsight we see His mighty Hand of provision. Start writing down your blessings each week and then review them at the end of the school year. You will be amazed at how much He has done when you look back over the year.

1:16 PM PRAYER

Please pray that the Fruit of the Spirit is evident in our classrooms. (Gal. 5:22)

QUOTE FOR THE DAY

In three words I can sum up everything I've learned about life: it goes on. **Robert Frost**

NOTES:
_____
_____
_____
_____
_____

Where we read the Bible with our brother and sisters in the public schools

DAILY PROMISES OF GOD
for educators

ISAIAH 54:10

NIV - *Though the mountains be shaken and the hills be removed, yet my unfailing love for you will not be shaken nor my covenant of peace be removed," says the Lord, who has compassion on you.*

RSV - *For the mountains may depart and the hills be removed but my steadfast love shall not depart from you, and my covenant of peace shall not be removed, says the Lord, who has compassion on you.*

KJV - *For the mountains shall depart, and the hills be removed; but my kindness shall not depart from thee, neither shall the covenant of my peace be removed, saith the Lord that hath mercy on thee.*

LB - *For the mountains may depart and the hills disappear, but my kindness shall not leave you. My promise of peace for you will never be broken, says the Lord who has mercy upon you.*

NOTE TO THE EDUCATOR

Our God is a covenant keeping God. Did you notice in these verses that He has made a covenant of peace? When school issues are in turmoil or your classroom is less than peaceful, call upon your covenant keeping God of peace. He has mercy, compassion and kindness towards us. He is the lifter of our heads. How do you tap into this peace? It's all about relationships. Think of the people that you enjoy the most and want to spend time with. That's relationship building. It works the same way with God. Learn to enjoy Him by spending time with Him. He is the Creator of all the beauty that surrounds us and each and every student that comes through our doors. Praise Him for His covenant of peace in prayer, praise and worship.

1:16 PM PRAYER

Please pray for the needs of the greeters at the front desk.

QUOTE FOR THE DAY

We the people tell the government what to do, it doesn't tell us. **Ronald Reagan**

NOTES:

_____

_____

_____

_____

_____

Where we read the Bible with our brother and sisters in the public schools

DAY 282

#iamachristianeducator

DAILY PROMISES OF GOD
for educators
ISAIAH 54:13

NIV - *All your children will be taught by the Lord, and great will be their peace.*

RSV - *All your sons shall be taught by the Lord, and great shall be the prosperity of your sons.*

KJV - *And all thy children shall be taught of the Lord; and great shall be the peace of thy children.*

LB - *And all your citizens shall be taught by me, and their prosperity shall be great.*

NOTE TO THE EDUCATOR

All the children will be taught by the Lord! This is a glimpse of eternity for sure. The result will be peace and prosperity. We are the children of the Lord now and we bring His hope to our schools. God's love and truth can transform a school. How can we do this legally and gracefully? How can we be Christian educators and be contagious? They must know us by our love. Our reputation for a cool head and merciful reaction to issues will always be undergirded with prayer and dependency upon the Word behind the scenes. We will ask Him for help in times of trouble and seek His Face for peace and prosperity in our classrooms. An educator guided by the Lord is a gift to any school.

1:16 PM PRAYER

Please pray for faithfulness to teach with integrity.

QUOTE FOR THE DAY

Being a politician is a poor profession. Being a public servant is a noble one. **Herbert Hoover**

NOTES:

_____
_____
_____
_____
_____

Where we read the Bible with our brother and sisters in the public schools

DAILY PROMISES OF GOD
for educators

ISAIAH 54:17

NIV - *No weapon forged against you will prevail, and you will refute every tongue that accuses you. This is the heritage of the servants of the Lord, and this is their vindication from me," declares the Lord.*

RSV - *No weapon that is fashioned against you shall prosper, and you shall confute every tongue that rises against you in judgment. This is the heritage of the servants of the Lord and their vindication from me, says the Lord."*

KJV - *No weapon that is formed against thee shall prosper; and every tongue that shall rise against thee in judgment thou shalt condemn. This is the heritage of the servants of the Lord, and their righteousness is of me, saith the Lord.*

LB - *But in that coming day, no weapon turned against you shall succeed, and you will have justice against every courtroom lie. This is the heritage of the servants of the Lord. This is the blessing I have given you, says the Lord.*

NOTE TO THE EDUCATOR

It's very different to be a Christian these days. From the outside looking in, we have been told that we are not wanted in our schools and public life. *"There's a separation of church and state, you know." (That is another topic for another time!)* As Christian educators, we see first hand the broken-hearted, the disabled, the poor and rejected. These children (and adults) need our compassion, mercy and grace that comes from honoring our Lord and King. In the public schools, we yearn to be His hands and feet to a campus of those who do not know Him, yet. We do not show Him with words, but with His love. May your efforts to show Jesus be wrapped with all His influence. His love is always the right way to go and the right thing to do. Be strong in Him, Christian educator, and win them over with His love.

1:16 PM PRAYER

Please pray to be an educator who is slow to anger. (Prov. 15:18)

QUOTE FOR THE DAY

A creative man is motivated by the desire to achieve, not by the desire to beat others. **Ayn Rand**

NOTES:
_____
_____
_____
_____
_____

DAY 84

#iamachristianeducator

Where we read the Bible with our brother and sisters in the public schools

DAILY PROMISES OF GOD
for educators
ISAIAH 55:10-11

NIV - *As the rain and the snow come down from heaven, and do not return to it without watering the earth and making it bud and flourish, so that it yields seed for the sower and bread for the eater, so is my word that goes out from my mouth: It will not return to me empty, but will accomplish what I desire and achieve the purpose for which I sent it.*

RSV - *For as the rain and the snow come down from heaven, and return not thither but water the earth, making it bring forth and sprout, giving seed to the sower and bread to the eater, so shall my word be that goes forth from my mouth; it shall not return to me empty, but it shall accomplish that which I purpose, and prosper in the thing for which I sent it.*

KJV - *For as the rain cometh down, and the snow from heaven, and returneth not thither, but watereth the earth, and maketh it bring forth and bud, that it may give seed to the sower, and bread to the eater: So shall my word be that goeth forth out of my mouth: it shall not return unto me void, but it shall accomplish that which I please, and it shall prosper in the thing whereto I sent it.*

LB - *As the rain and snow come down from heaven and stay upon the ground to water the earth, and cause the grain to grow and to produce seed for the farmer and bread for the hungry, so also is my word. I send it out, and it always produces fruit. It shall accomplish all I want it to and prosper everywhere I send it.*

NOTE TO THE EDUCATOR

In days of old, God spoke through His prophets, but now He has made Jesus Christ His Prophet and Priest. He speaks through His Word – the Bible. Its words do not return void. It is a gift to be in the Word of God each day. Around the Word in 180 Days is designed to help you, the busy educator, to be in the Word each day. It is an appetizer to your own meal into the Bread of Life. Reading, meditating and listening to the Word of God is nutrition. Just as you wouldn't go without eating all day, you shouldn't go without being in the Word of God each day as a Christian. Share how you keep yourself nourished in the comment area of our website today. It may encourage your brothers and sisters to be in the Word. www.aw180days.com

1:16 PM PRAYER

Please pray to be an educator who finds joy in giving an apt reply and a timely word. (Prov. 15:23)

QUOTE FOR THE DAY

It does not matter how slowly you go as long as you do not stop. **Confucius**

NOTES:

_____

_____

_____

_____

Where we read the Bible with our brother and sisters in the public schools

DAILY PROMISES OF GOD
for educators

ISAIAH 58:7-8

NIV - *Is it not to share your food with the hungry and to provide the poor wanderer with shelter—when you see the naked, to clothe them, and not to turn away from your own flesh and blood? Then your light will break forth like the dawn, and your healing will quickly appear; then your righteousness will go before you, and the glory of the Lord will be your rear guard.*

RSV - *Is it not to share your bread with the hungry, and bring the homeless poor into your house; when you see the naked, to cover him, and not to hide yourself from your own flesh? Then shall your light break forth like the dawn, and your healing shall spring up speedily; your righteousness shall go before you, the glory of the Lord shall be your rear guard.*

KJV - *Is it not to deal thy bread to the hungry, and that thou bring the poor that are cast out to thy house? when thou seest the naked, that thou cover him; and that thou hide not thyself from thine own flesh? Then shall thy light break forth as the morning, and thine health shall spring forth speedily: and thy righteousness shall go before thee; the glory of the Lord shall be thy reward.*

LB - *I want you to share your food with the hungry and bring right into your own homes those who are helpless, poor, and destitute. Clothe those who are cold, and don't hide from relatives who need your help. If you do these things, God will shed his own glorious light upon you. He will heal you; your godliness will lead you forward, goodness will be a shield before you, and the glory of the Lord will protect you from behind.*

NOTE TO THE EDUCATOR

Do we have the poor, destitute and helpless in America? Yes indeed, and we serve them every day in school. How can we go beyond Social Studies, Math or Science for these precious children? Is it our job? If you are a Christian in the public schools, it may be why you have been placed in such a position. Ask God to help you identify the needs of the poorest of your students. Being discreet about it will give you the ability to truly help. Ask others on your campus to get together to determine the best means of provision. Perhaps you can start a clothing shop in your school for those children to "earn" a coupon to go shopping. Every school is unique, but all schools have students with needs. Let's be the ones to serve them.

1:16 PM PRAYER

Please pray for kindness to spread contagiously.

QUOTE FOR THE DAY

You are never too old to set another goal or to dream a new dream.   **C.S. Lewis**

NOTES:

_____

_____

_____

_____

DAY 689

#iamachristianeducator

 Where we read the Bible with our brother and sisters in the public schools

DAILY PROMISES OF GOD
for educators

ISAIAH 64:4

NIV - *Since ancient times no one has heard, no ear has perceived, no eye has seen any God besides you, who acts on behalf of those who wait for him.*

RSV - *From of old no one has heard or perceived by the ear, no eye has seen a God besides thee, who works for those who wait for him.*

KJV - *For since the beginning of the world men have not heard, nor perceived by the ear, neither hath the eye seen, O God, beside thee, what he hath prepared for him that waiteth for him.*

LB - *For since the world began no one has seen or heard of such a God as ours, who works for those who wait for him!*

NOTE TO THE EDUCATOR

Waiting on God can seem like an eternity. We want what we want and we want it right now. That's not God's way. He said that a day is like a thousand years to Him. (2nd Peter 3:8) As we petition our Lord for the needs of our students, our colleagues and our school community, it may seem that He is not listening. Take heart. He is always listening to our prayers and always working on our behalf. Always. There is no one like Him. Continue steadfastly in prayer being ever watchful in it with thanksgiving. (Col. 4:2) While you are waiting, give thanks that He is a God of promises, a covenant keeping God and One Who works for those who wait on Him.

1:16 PM PRAYER

Please pray for peace for students and/or colleagues who are stressed.

QUOTE FOR THE DAY

The secret of getting ahead is getting started. **Anonymous**

NOTES:
_____
_____
_____
_____
_____

DAY 87

#iamachristianeducator

Where we read the Bible with our brother and sisters in the public schools

DAILY PROMISES OF GOD
for educators

ISAIAH 65:24

NIV - *Before they call I will answer; while they are still speaking I will hear.*

RSV - *Before they call I will answer, while they are yet speaking I will hear.*

KJV - *And it shall come to pass, that before they call, I will answer; and while they are yet speaking, I will hear.*

LB - *I will answer them before they even call to me. While they are still talking to me about their needs, I will go ahead and answer their prayers!*

NOTE TO THE EDUCATOR

I stand amazed by how God answers prayer. Just yesterday we were wondering if God listens to our prayers. Without a plan, the next promise in His word is that He <u>will</u> answer and that even before we are speaking He will hear! The Word of God is His answer to everything in life. No matter what you are wondering about, He is the Answer. The more we read the Word, the more we want to be in it. Can you read the Bible in school? Of course you can! The only restriction is reading it devotionally. The students can read it any time as long as it does not interrupt instruction. As a Christian educator, it is legal to have a Bible on your desk and in fact, you will find the Bible in the 200 section of your media center. Being in His word daily reaps incredible benefits that are eternal.

1:16 PM PRAYER

Please pray for peace on earth, good will towards man. (Luke 2:14 KJV)

QUOTE FOR THE DAY

There is only one corner of the universe you can be certain of improving, and that's your own self.
Unknown

NOTES:
_____
_____
_____
_____
_____

Where we read the Bible with our brother and sisters in the public schools

#iamachristianeducator

DAILY PROMISES OF GOD
for educators

JEREMIAH 1:5

NIV - *Before I formed you in the womb I knew you, before you were born I set you apart; I appointed you as a prophet to the nations.*

RSV - *Before I formed you in the womb I knew you, and before you were born I consecrated you; I appointed you a prophet to the nations.*

KJV - *Before I formed thee in the belly I knew thee; and before thou camest forth out of the womb I sanctified thee, and I ordained thee a prophet unto the nations.*

LB - *I knew you before you were formed within your mother's womb; before you were born I sanctified you and appointed you as my spokesman to the world.*

NOTE TO THE EDUCATOR

These are powerful words spoken to Jeremiah by His Creator! What do you think God would be saying to you if you could hear His voice? It may be something like this: Before you were born, dear Christian, I formed you in your mother's womb to be an educator. I set you apart to be the light and the salt for Me in the public schools. There are really only two ways to become an educator. It's a job you choose and you put your time in, collect your paycheck and do your best. Or, it is a high calling. You were chosen by God to be an educator. Every part of your being cries out to serve the students and represent Him well. Be encouraged dear friend, you have a high calling given to you by the Creator Himself.

1:16 PM PRAYER

Please pray for the power to be prayerfully dependent educators.

QUOTE FOR THE DAY

In the end, it's not the years in your life that count. It's the life in your years. **Abraham Lincoln**

NOTES:

_____
_____
_____
_____
_____

Where we read the Bible with our brother and sisters in the public schools

DAILY PROMISES OF GOD
for educators

JEREMIAH 17:14

NIV - *Heal me, Lord, and I will be healed; save me and I will be saved, for you are the one I praise.*

RSV - *Heal me, O Lord, and I shall be healed; save me, and I shall be saved; for thou art my praise.*

KJV - *Heal me, O Lord, and I shall be healed; save me, and I shall be saved: for thou art my praise.*

LB - *Lord, you alone can heal me, you alone can save, and my praises are for you alone.*

NOTE TO THE EDUCATOR

We Christians share an amazing joy. He heals us. He saves us. He alone does all things for us. What an advantage it is to be a Christian educator. When we need creativity to keep our students engaged, we call upon the Creator. When we need help with course correction and redesign, we call upon our Forgiver. When we need a reminder of how good we have it, we count our blessings. When we do, our perspective on our hard things is softened. Make it a practice to give thanks each day. Before you leave your campus, try to remember to praise Him for these things. I praise Him for dedicated educators. I praise Him for administrators that lead. I praise Him for students who are made in His image.

1:16 PM PRAYER

Please pray that the words of our mouths and the meditations of our hearts are pleasing to God (Ps. 19:14)

QUOTE FOR THE DAY

I have found that if you love life, life will love you back. **Arthur Rubenstein**

NOTES:

_____

_____

_____

_____

_____

DAY 90

#iamachristianeducator

 Where we read the Bible with our brother and sisters in the public schools

DAILY PROMISES OF GOD
for educators
JEREMIAH 24:6-7

NIV - *My eyes will watch over them for their good, and I will bring them back to this land. I will build them up and not tear them down; I will plant them and not uproot them. I will give them a heart to know me, that I am the Lord. They will be my people, and I will be their God, for they will return to me with all their heart.*

RSV - *I will set my eyes upon them for good, and I will bring them back to this land. I will build them up, and not tear them down; I will plant them, and not uproot them. I will give them a heart to know that I am the Lord; and they shall be my people and I will be their God, for they shall return to me with their whole heart.*

KJV - *For I will set mine eyes upon them for good, and I will bring them again to this land: and I will build them, and not pull them down; and I will plant them, and not pluck them up. And I will give them an heart to know me, that I am the Lord: and they shall be my people, and I will be their God: for they shall return unto me with their whole heart.*

LB - *I will see that they are well treated, and I will bring them back here again. I will help them and not hurt them; I will plant them and not pull them up. I will give them hearts that respond to me. They shall be my people and I will be their God, for they shall return to me with great joy.*

NOTE TO THE EDUCATOR

God has called out to His people all throughout the Bible to return to Him. He has always sought their good, and desires that we worship Him with our whole heart. Don't you just yearn for your students, colleagues and school community to know the Lord with their whole heart? The majority of our human connections at school are non-believers. We have something so precious and such a hope for tomorrow that we need to be contagious. We need to walk in a way that others wonder what makes us tick. We need to represent ourselves in such a way that our sphere of influence wants what we have. Let us be always mindful of how we treat each other, each and every day because they are always watching.

1:16 PM PRAYER

Please pray that self-control is modeled in our classrooms.

QUOTE FOR THE DAY

Creativity is intelligence having fun. **Albert Einstein**

NOTES:
_____
_____
_____
_____
_____

Where we read the Bible with our brother and sisters in the public schools

DAILY PROMISES OF GOD
for educators

JEREMIAH 29:11-13

NIV - *For I know the plans I have for you, declares the Lord, plans to prosper you and not to harm you, plans to give you hope and a future. Then you will call on me and come and pray to me, and I will listen to you. You will seek me and find me when you seek me with all your heart.*

RSV - *For I know the plans I have for you, says the Lord, plans for welfare and not for evil, to give you a future and a hope. Then you will call upon me and come and pray to me, and I will hear you. You will seek me and find me; when you seek me with all your heart.*

KJV - *For I know the thoughts that I think toward you, saith the Lord, thoughts of peace, and not of evil, to give you an expected end. Then shall ye call upon me, and ye shall go and pray unto me, and I will hearken unto you. And ye shall seek me, and find me, when ye shall search for me with all your heart.*

LB - *For I know the plans I have for you, says the Lord. They are plans for good and not for evil, to give you a future and a hope. In those days when you pray, I will listen. You will find me when you seek me, if you look for me in earnest.*

NOTE TO THE EDUCATOR

These words to Jeremiah are a reminder to us that we serve a mighty God Who is listening to our prayers. He desires that we are successful. He yearns for our faithfulness and He promises to be listening if we seek Him with our whole heart. Do you remember the wholeheartedness of the first day of school in your first position at school? You definitely jumped in wholeheartedly and there's no doubt you prayed for His help. Can we still come to school wholeheartedly, be totally in the game and seek Him in prayer? It is His promise that we will find Him when we seek Him with our whole heart. Call upon Him daily with every ounce of your being. Ask for renewed enthusiasm and excitement for learning.

1:16 PM PRAYER

Please pray for the faith to trust God's absolute sovereignty over our school communities.

QUOTE FOR THE DAY

The surest way not to fail is to determine to succeed. **Richard Brinsley Sheridan**

NOTES:

_____

_____

_____

_____

_____

DAY 92

#iamachristianeducator

Where we read the Bible with our brother and sisters in the public schools

DAILY PROMISES OF GOD
for educators

JEREMIAH 31:3

DAY 93

NIV - *The Lord appeared to us in the past, saying: I have loved you with an everlasting love; I have drawn you with unfailing kindness.*

RSV - *The Lord appeared to him from afar. I have loved you with an everlasting love; therefore I have continued my faithfulness to you.*

KJV - *The Lord hath appeared of old unto me, saying, Yea, I have loved thee with an everlasting love: therefore with lovingkindness have I drawn thee.*

LB - *For long ago the Lord had said to Israel: I have loved you, O my people, with an everlasting love; with loving-kindness I have drawn you to me.*

NOTE TO THE EDUCATOR

Lovingkindness is a characteristic of a Christian educator. There is little or no professional development on love in the classroom unfortunately. Why not? Everyone knows that love always wins, that love conquers all, so why aren't we taught about loving our students and colleagues more? We can be very influential in the dialogue of love and in the modeling of love because He loved us first. Committing to loving our students and colleagues is a Christian responsibility. Begin by choosing three specific people that you are going to go out of your way to love on this year. Try one student, one colleague and one administrator or paraprofessional. Don't tell them what you are doing, but be intentional about displaying love for them. Do it for no other reason, but to display the love of our Lord upon them with random acts of kindness throughout the rest of the school year.

1:16 PM PRAYER

Please pray that we can pause in difficult times and ask, *"What would Jesus do?"*

QUOTE FOR THE DAY

The best way to predict the future is to create it. **Abraham Lincoln**

NOTES:
_____
_____
_____
_____
_____

#iamachristianeducator

Where we read the Bible with our brother and sisters in the public schools

DAILY PROMISES OF GOD
for educators

JEREMIAH 33:3

NIV - *Call to me and I will answer you and tell you great and unsearchable things you do not know.*

RSV - *Call to me and I will answer you, and will tell you great and hidden things which you have not known.*

KJV - *Call unto me, and I will answer thee, and show thee great and mighty things, which thou knowest not.*

LB - *Ask me and I will tell you some remarkable secrets about what is going to happen here.*

NOTE TO THE EDUCATOR

Is there any doubt that God wants us to pray? He has repeatedly told us to call upon Him and He will hear our cry. Prayer is the Christian educator's greatest tool. It is more important than a well-managed classroom. It is more important than lesson plans. It takes higher priority than faculty meetings and it is certainly more important than our planning periods. We have all been a part of a PLC (Professional Learning Community), but have you considered this vital PLC (Prayer Life Community)? This private PLC can undergird all other PLCs by calling out to God to bless our plans, our creativity and our success. The Prayer Life Community can meet before or after school on a regular basis to pray for the needs of the whole school community. There is no doubt that a campus that is being prayed for is a school community that will succeed.

1:16 PM PRAYER

Please pray for the needs of the testing coordinators.

QUOTE FOR THE DAY

There is no substitute for hard work. **Thomas Edison**

NOTES:

_____

_____

_____

_____

_____

Where we read the Bible with our brother and sisters in the public schools

DAILY PROMISES OF GOD
for educators
JEREMIAH 49:11

NIV - *Leave your fatherless children; I will keep them alive. Your widows too can depend on me.*

RSV - *Leave your fatherless children, I will keep them alive; and let your widows trust in me.*

KJV - *Leave thy fatherless children, I will preserve them alive; and let thy widows trust in me.*

LB - *But I will preserve your fatherless children who remain, and let your widows depend upon me.*

NOTE TO THE EDUCATOR

This promise was made during a time of war. We have been so blessed in this generation to not be directly affected by the ravages of war, but we certainly do see the results of fatherless children and widows. Let's make a special effort to go out of our way today to show some love to any widows or widowers on our campus. First pray for them and then consider writing a small note to them. It is super special to receive a card instead of email! Do you know which students are fatherless or who are being raised by a single parent or grandparent? Seek to know who these students are and look in on them. Finding out how they are doing and wanting to serve them is Jesus's way. Each situation will be delicately different. Handle with care.

1:16 PM PRAYER

Please pray that we may be a comfort to those students who are hurting.

QUOTE FOR THE DAY

I'm not afraid of death; I just don't want to be there when it happens. **Woody Allen**

NOTES:
_____
_____
_____
_____
_____

Where we read the Bible with our brother and sisters in the public schools

DAILY PROMISES OF GOD
for educators

EZEKIEL 36:26-27

NIV - *I will give you a new heart and put a new spirit in you; I will remove from you your heart of stone and give you a heart of flesh. And I will put my Spirit in you and move you to follow my decrees and be careful to keep my laws.*

RSV - *A new heart I will give you, and a new spirit I will put within you; and I will take out of your flesh the heart of stone and give you a heart of flesh. And I will put my spirit within you, and cause you to walk in my statutes and be careful to observe my ordinances.*

KJV - *A new heart also will I give you, and a new spirit will I put within you: and I will take away the stony heart out of your flesh, and I will give you an heart of flesh. And I will put my spirit within you, and cause you to walk in my statutes, and ye shall keep my judgments, and do them.*

LB - *And I will give you a new heart—I will give you new and right desires—and put a new spirit within you. I will take out your stony hearts of sin and give you new hearts of love. And I will put my Spirit within you so that you will obey my laws and do whatever I command.*

NOTE TO THE EDUCATOR

This promise is our hope as Christians. We live for the kingdom where all God's children will have a new heart. Can you imagine what that would mean in a classroom? Teachers and students with new hearts, hearts of love, will do everything and anything to please and comfort. Learning would never be a struggle or problem. Rebellion will not exist. There would be no need for discipline! As Christians in the public school, it is our high calling to model heaven on earth in a very small way. Pray for new hearts for your students. Pray for hearts of flesh for your colleagues as conflicts arise. Model forgiveness and graciousness in your relationships with the guidance and power of the Holy Spirit.

1:16 PM PRAYER

Please pray that the message of Martin Luther King, Jr.'s "*I Have a Dream*" speech is heartfelt by our students and colleagues.

QUOTE FOR THE DAY

So many books, so little time. **Frank Zappa**

NOTES:

_____

_____

_____

_____

_____

Where we read the Bible with our brother and sisters in the public schools

DAILY PROMISES OF GOD
for educators

ZEPHANIAH 3:17

NIV - *The Lord your God is with you, the Mighty Warrior who saves. He will take great delight in you; in his love he will no longer rebuke you, but will rejoice over you with singing.*

RSV - *The Lord your God is in your midst, a warrior who gives victory; he will rejoice over you with gladness, he will renew you in his love; he will exult over you with loud singing.*

KJV - *The Lord thy God in the midst of thee is mighty; he will save, he will rejoice over thee with joy; he will rest in his love, he will joy over thee with singing.*

LB - *For the Lord your God has arrived to live among you. He is a mighty Savior. He will give you victory. He will rejoice over you with great gladness; he will love you and not accuse you. Is that a joyous choir I hear? No, it is the Lord himself exulting over you in happy song.*

NOTE TO THE EDUCATOR

Our God is a precious God. Can you see this picture of God singing over us? What a God of joy! What a pleasant reminder. If God sings over His children in delight, why wouldn't we sing over our students? Think of a song that really makes you happy and one you can sing from memory. If you can't think of one, find one. Make it the song of your heart for the rest of this school year. When a student is troubling you or has personal issues, sing your song of joy over them in your heart. If you are really brave, make your song your signal to your students when you want to bring them back on task. Music is a powerful healer and is the common language of all God's children. Even if you are not a singer, you can make a joyful noise!

1:16 PM PRAYER

Please pray that our students see us as ambassadors of Christ without using words.

QUOTE FOR THE DAY

Anyone who thinks sitting in church can make you a Christian must also think that sitting in a garage can make you a car. **Garrison Keillor**

NOTES:

_____

_____

_____

_____

_____

Where we read the Bible with our brother and sisters in the public schools

DAILY PROMISES OF GOD
for educators

MALACHI 3:8-10

NIV - *Will a mere mortal rob God? Yet you rob me. But you ask, "How are we robbing you?" In tithes and offerings. You are under a curse—your whole nation—because you are robbing me. Bring the whole tithe into the storehouse, that there may be food in my house. Test me in this," says the Lord Almighty, "and see if I will not throw open the floodgates of heaven and pour out so much blessing that there will not be room enough to store it.*

RSV - *Will man rob God? Yet you are robbing me. But you say, "How are we robbing thee?" In your tithes and offerings. You are cursed with a curse, for you are robbing me; the whole nation of you. Bring the full tithes into the storehouse, that there may be food in my house; and thereby put me to the test," says the Lord of hosts, "if I will not open the windows of heaven for you and pour down for you an overflowing blessing."*

KJV - *Will a man rob God? Yet ye have robbed me. But ye say, Wherein have we robbed thee? In tithes and offerings. Ye are cursed with a curse: for ye have robbed me, even this whole nation. Bring ye all the tithes into the storehouse, that there may be meat in mine house, and prove me now herewith, saith the Lord of hosts, if I will not open you the windows of heaven, and pour you out a blessing, that there shall not be room enough to receive it.*

LB - *Will a man rob God? Surely not! And yet you have robbed me. "What do you mean? When did we ever rob you? You have robbed me of the tithes and offerings due me. And so the awesome curse of God is cursing you, for your whole nation has been robbing me. Bring all the tithes into the storehouse so that there will be food enough in my Temple; if you do, I will open up the windows of heaven for you and pour out a blessing so great you won't have room enough to take it in! Try it! Let me prove it to you!*

NOTE TO THE EDUCATOR

There is no other place in Scripture where God challenges us to prove Him and test Him. Can you imagine how wealthy this nation would be if everyone paid their tithe? Our churches would be overflowing with resources to help the poor and needy. We would be blessed as a nation also. Can you imagine if everyone's taxes were 10% - no forms to fill out, no loop holes, no deductions? Our schools would be fully funded, our libraries would be stacked and our needs would be totally met. I realize it is only a dream, but it is a reality to those who have seen the miracle of tithing in their lives.

1:16 PM PRAYER

Please pray to remember that the Holy Spirit is our advisor.

QUOTE FOR THE DAY

For every minute you are angry you lose sixty seconds of happiness.   **Ralph Waldo Emerson**

NOTES:
___
___
___
___
___

Where we read the Bible with our brother and sisters in the public schools

DAILY PROMISES OF GOD
for educators

MALACHI 4:6

NIV - *He will turn the hearts of the parents to their children, and the hearts of the children to their parents; or else I will come and strike the land with total destruction.*

RSV - *And he will turn the hearts of fathers to their children and the hearts of children to their fathers, lest I come and smite the land with a curse.*

KJV - *And he shall turn the heart of the fathers to the children, and the heart of the children to their fathers, lest I come and smite the earth with a curse.*

LB - *His preaching will bring fathers and children together again, to be of one mind and heart, for they will know that if they do not repent, I will come and utterly destroy their land.*

NOTE TO THE EDUCATOR

Who is this mighty preacher? Who is this powerful prophet who can turn the hearts of the fathers to their children? Christ alone can turn hearts. Although the promise of turning hearts to the children is future, there is a present element. When unbelievers come to know Jesus, their hearts are turned. Pray for those who do not know Jesus on your campus. Pray that they will come to know Him in a transformational manner. Pray that He invades their whole being so that their hearts will be turned to Him. If the hearts of the fathers were turned to the children, the majority of our public school and societal issues would cease. We need fathers in our homes, but most of all we need Jesus!

1:16 PM PRAYER

Please pray that we remember God's wisdom. (Romans 11:33)

QUOTE FOR THE DAY

That which does not kill us makes us stronger. **Friedrich Nietzsche**

NOTES:

_____
_____
_____
_____
_____

Where we read the Bible with our brother and sisters in the public schools

DAILY PROMISES OF GOD
for educators

MATTHEW 5:4

NIV - *Blessed are those who mourn, for they will be comforted.*

RSV - *Blessed are those who mourn, for they shall be comforted.*

KJV - *Blessed are they that mourn: for they shall be comforted.*

LB - *Those who mourn are fortunate! for they shall be comforted.*

NOTE TO THE EDUCATOR

Do you have any students or colleagues who are mourning the death of a loved one? In any school community, we unfortunately experience death at some point during the year. It's a part of life. We need to fill in the gap for those who are mourning. Bring a meal, share some time with them to supply their needs. Listen. Comfort them with physical needs. Cover their spiritual needs by praying for their families by name. Find out who needs prayers by asking how you can pray for them. Then pray prayers of comfort for the grieving. It's a difficult time and the love of Jesus Christ is the only healer.

1:16 PM PRAYER

Please pray that every day we are approachable, available, affectionate, authentic and authoritative in all that we do and encounter.

QUOTE FOR THE DAY

The man who does not read has no advantage over the man who cannot read. **Mark Twain**

NOTES:

_____

_____

_____

_____

_____

Where we read the Bible with our brother and sisters in the public schools

DAILY PROMISES OF GOD
for educators

MATTHEW 5:6

NIV - *Blessed are those who hunger and thirst for righteousness, for they will be filled.*

RSV - *Blessed are those who hunger and thirst for righteousness, for they shall be satisfied.*

KJV - *Blessed are they which do hunger and thirst after righteousness: for they shall be filled.*

LB - *Happy are those who long to be just and good, for they shall be completely satisfied.*

NOTE TO THE EDUCATOR

Righteousness is a word that is rarely used in a positive manner these days. Those who do not know Christ, look at righteousness as self-righteousness and want little or nothing to do with others who think too much about themselves. However, Godly righteousness is what we would love to attain, yet know that it is impossible without His saving grace. Once you know that Jesus is Lord and Savior, and you know that you are saved because of what He did, then it is only natural to seek to be righteous, doing things God's way, because we want to please Him. Set the standard for your classroom to be a righteous place. Hunger and thirst to bring an environment of love, joy and peace His way and He will help you. That is satisfaction. May God give you the ability to seek righteousness that He may receive all the glory.

1:16 PM PRAYER

Please pray for the needs of our crossing guards.

QUOTE FOR THE DAY

If you don't stand for something you will fall for anything. **Gordon A. Eadie**

NOTES:

_____

_____

_____

_____

_____

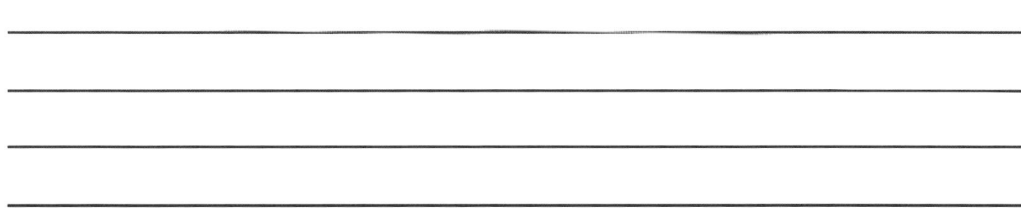

Where we read the Bible with our brother and sisters in the public schools

DAY 101

#iamachristianeducator

DAILY PROMISES OF GOD
for educators

MATTHEW 5:7

DAY 102

NIV - *Blessed are the merciful, for they will be shown mercy.*

RSV - *Blessed are the merciful, for they shall obtain mercy.*

KJV - *Blessed are the merciful: for they shall obtain mercy.*

LB - *Happy are the kind and merciful, for they shall be shown mercy.*

NOTE TO THE EDUCATOR

Paybacks are so sweet when they are done God's way. The natural way of paybacks occurs daily in the classroom and school yard. *"I'll get you back." "He did it first." "It wasn't me. I was just….."* Younger students are tattletales. Older students take things into their own hands. Adults are much more vindictive in their paybacks. Christian educators, we have been called to payback God's way. When someone hurts us, our Lord Jesus told us to pray for them. (Matt. 5:44) After praying for them, we need to show mercy to them. Place yourselves in their shoes and ask God to help you see. Forgive that colleague today for that offense and be merciful to them. It is God's promise that He will be merciful to you. That's awesome motivation.

1:16 PM PRAYER

Please pray that we learn how to accept each others' differences.

QUOTE FOR THE DAY

There are only two ways to live your life. One is as though nothing is a miracle. The other is as though everything is a miracle. **Albert Einstein**

NOTES:

_____
_____
_____
_____
_____

#iamachristianeducator

Where we read the Bible with our brother and sisters in the public schools

DAILY PROMISES OF GOD
for educators

MATTHEW 5:8

DAY 103

NIV - *Blessed are the pure in heart, for they will see God.*

RSV - *Blessed are the pure in heart, for they shall see God.*

KJV - *Blessed are the pure in heart: for they shall see God.*

LB - *Happy are those whose hearts are pure, for they shall see God.*

NOTE TO THE EDUCATOR

How's your heart? Is it pure? Does it need an extreme makeover? We serve a God of second chances. We can be like David and ask God to create in us a new heart. (Ps. 51:10). We can ask Him to renew a right spirit within us. If your heart is not right, nothing else is really right. We can't teach properly, we can't serve our students with integrity or be a gift to our colleagues. Getting your heart right with God is the highest priority of the school year. It needs refreshing, retuning and cleansing daily from the Fountain of Life. With a pure heart, we are able to be a contagious Christian and bless those with whom we interact each day. These are the words of **Ps. 51:10-12** for a model - *Create in me a pure heart, O God, and renew a steadfast spirit within me. Do not cast me from your presence or take your Holy Spirit from me. Restore to me the joy of your salvation and grant me a willing spirit, to sustain me.*

1:16 PM PRAYER

Please pray Eph. 4:26 In your anger, do not sin. Do not let the sun go down while you are still angry.

QUOTE FOR THE DAY

A friend is someone who knows all about you and still loves you. **Elbert Hubbard**

NOTES:

_____
_____
_____
_____
_____

#iamachristianeducator

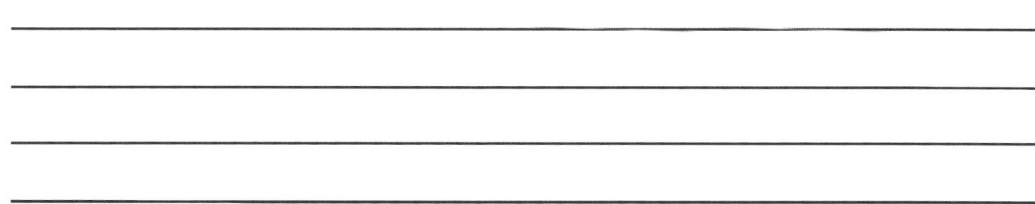

Where we read the Bible with our brother and sisters in the public schools

DAILY PROMISES OF GOD
for educators

MATTHEW 5:9

NIV - *Blessed are the peacemakers, for they will be called children of God.*

RSV - *Blessed are the peacemakers, for they shall be called sons of God.*

KJV - *Blessed are the peacemakers: for they shall be called the children of God.*

LB - *Happy are those who strive for peace—they shall be called the sons of God.*

NOTE TO THE EDUCATOR

Be a peacemaker. Be the one who stands in the gap. Who do you think of when you think of a peacemaker? Dr. Martin Luther King, Jr. or Mother Teresa? Is there someone on your campus that is a peacemaker? Peacemaker should be synonymous with Christian. The best definition of peacemaker I found was on *His Peace Upon Us* blog. *"A peacemaker is someone who experiences the peace of God (Phil. 4:7) because he is at peace (Roms. 5:1) with the God of peace (Phil. 4:9) through the Prince of Peace (Isa. 9:6), who, indeed is our peace (Eph. 2:14), and who therefore seeks to live at peace with all others (Roms. 12:18) and proclaims the gospel of peace (Eph. 6:15) so that others might have joy and peace in believing (Roms. 15:13)."* We are His sons and daughters, we bear the title Peacemaker. Let us strive to bring peace to our campuses by the power of His Spirit.

1:16 PM PRAYER

Please pray that the students desire to be successful in their academic pursuits.

QUOTE FOR THE DAY

No one can make you feel inferior without your consent. **Eleanor Roosevelt**

NOTES:
_____
_____
_____
_____
_____

DAY 104

#iamachristianeducator

Where we read the Bible with our brother and sisters in the public schools

DAILY PROMISES OF GOD
for educators

MATTHEW 6:8

NIV - *Do not be like them, for your Father knows what you need before you ask him.*

RSV - *Do not be like them, for your Father knows what you need before you ask him.*

KJV - *Be not ye therefore like unto them: for your Father knoweth what things ye have need of, before ye ask him.*

LB - *Remember, your Father knows exactly what you need even before you ask him!*

NOTE TO THE EDUCATOR

If our Father already knows what we need before we even ask Him then why do we have to ask? Every educator, parent or grandparent can easily understand this position if you think about it. When our students are most curious, they are asking questions. We already know the answers because we have prepared the lesson, but we encourage them to ask in order for them to be engaged in the lesson and to make sure their needs are met. Parents and grandparents will allow and encourage their child to ask for what they need to make sure they really need something and it's not just a want. Go confidently before your Father today for your needs. He just wants to hear from you. He's so generous and He not only knows what we need, He knows what's best for us.

1:16 PM PRAYER

Please pray that the students will be overwhelmed with a sense of gratitude.

QUOTE FOR THE DAY

The study of the Bible is a post-graduate course in the richest library of human experience.
Hebert Hoover

NOTES:
_____
_____
_____
_____
_____

Where we read the Bible with our brother and sisters in the public schools

DAILY PROMISES OF GOD
for educators

MATTHEW 6:25-26

DAY 106

NIV - *Therefore I tell you, do not worry about your life, what you will eat or drink; or about your body, what you will wear. Is not life more than food, and the body more than clothes? Look at the birds of the air; they do not sow or reap or store away in barns, and yet your heavenly Father feeds them. Are you not much more valuable than they?*

RSV - *Therefore I tell you, do not be anxious about your life, what you shall eat or what you shall drink, nor about your body, what you shall put on. Is not life more than food, and the body more than clothing? Look at the birds of the air: they neither sow nor reap nor gather into barns, and yet your heavenly Father feeds them. Are you not of more value than they?*

KJV - *Therefore I say unto you, Take no thought for your life, what ye shall eat, or what ye shall drink; nor yet for your body, what ye shall put on. Is not the life more than meat, and the body than raiment? Behold the fowls of the air: for they sow not, neither do they reap, nor gather into barns; yet your heavenly Father feedeth them. Are ye not much better than they?*

LB - *So my counsel is: Don't worry about things—food, drink, and clothes. For you already have life and a body—and they are far more important than what to eat and wear. Look at the birds! They don't worry about what to eat—they don't need to sow or reap or store up food— for your heavenly Father feeds them. And you are far more valuable to him than they are.*

NOTE TO THE EDUCATOR

You are far more valuable than the birds of the air! Your Father in heaven is guarding you and watching over you in your school. Welcome Him each day. Praise Him for His protection and loving arms. Your students are more valuable to Him than curriculum or standards. He loves them as He loves you. Thank Him for giving you the students He has placed in your care this year. Value them as He does, yes, even the ones that drive you crazy. They may be just the reason you are there. Allow yourself to be valuable in His eyes. Embrace the value of each of the students that you meet on your campus. He cares for them more than anything.

1:16 PM PRAYER

Please pray to see our colleagues as fearfully and wonderfully made by Him.

QUOTE FOR THE DAY

Logic will get you from A to Z; imagination will get you anywhere. **Albert Einstein**

NOTES:
_____
_____
_____
_____
_____

#iamachristianeducator

 Where we read the Bible with our brother and sisters in the public schools

DAILY PROMISES OF GOD
for educators

MATTHEW 6:31-33

NIV - *So do not worry, saying, 'What shall we eat?' or 'What shall we drink?' or 'What shall we wear?' For the pagans run after all these things, and your heavenly Father knows that you need them. But seek first his kingdom and his righteousness, and all these things will be given to you as well.*

RSV - *Therefore do not be anxious, saying, 'What shall we eat?' or 'What shall we drink?' or 'What shall we wear?' For the Gentiles seek all these things; and your heavenly Father knows that you need them all. But seek first his kingdom and his righteousness, and all these things shall be yours as well.*

KJV - *Therefore take no thought, saying, What shall we eat? or, What shall we drink? or, Wherewithal shall we be clothed? (For after all these things do the Gentiles seek:) for your heavenly Father knoweth that ye have need of all these things. But seek ye first the kingdom of God, and his righteousness; and all these things shall be added unto you.*

LB - *So don't worry at all about having enough food and clothing. Why be like the heathen? For they take pride in all these things and are deeply concerned about them. But your heavenly Father already knows perfectly well that you need them, and he will give them to you if you give him first place in your life and live as he wants you to.*

NOTE TO THE EDUCATOR

Sometimes the school day is like running on a hamster wheel. The rapid pace of the day and the innumerable things to do can get anyone flustered. The remedy is always in the Word of God. Seek first His kingdom. Give Him first place in your life. First is first. Speak to Him as soon as you wake up. Give him praise on your drive to school. Begin a **First Step** prayer. These prayers are special because they remove the burden of worry as you get to school. The moment you take the **first step** out of your vehicle, begin to pray about the day's needs. Give Him your priority list, give Him your requests for others and ask Him to bless your campus. In these few moments to the front door, you have put the kingdom first and you can relax because He has promised to fulfill your needs.

1:16 PM PRAYER

Please pray for the needs of our substitute teachers.

QUOTE FOR THE DAY

Today a reader, tomorrow a leader. **Margaret Fuller**

NOTES:

_____

_____

_____

_____

_____

DAY 107

#iamachristianeducator

 *Where we read the Bible with our brother and sisters in the public schools*

DAILY PROMISES OF GOD
for educators

MATTHEW 7:1

NIV - *Do not judge, or you too will be judged.*

RSV - *Judge not, that you be not judged.*

KJV - *Judge not, that ye be not judged.*

LB - *Don't criticize, and then you won't be criticized.*

NOTE TO THE EDUCATOR

One of the most judgmental places on any school campus is the faculty lounge. The tendency is to talk about the students or policies or random happenings at school, but as a Christian educator we have the opportunity to be a light. If you find yourself in a position of gossip, criticism or judgment, let these words of Jesus ring out in your spirit. Guide the conversation. Change the subject. Tell about some good news that happened to a colleague or student. Turn the discussion around. You may be accused of wearing rose-colored glasses, but it will help others see the difference without judgment.

1:16 PM PRAYER

Please pray that we express God's love through patience and kindness.

QUOTE FOR THE DAY

Quality is not an act, it is a habit. **Aristotle**

NOTES:
_____
_____
_____
_____
_____

Where we read the Bible with our brother and sisters in the public schools

DAY 108

#iamachristianeducator

DAILY PROMISES OF GOD
for educators

MATTHEW 8:16-17

NIV - *When evening came, many who were demon-possessed were brought to him, and he drove out the spirits with a word and healed all the sick. This was to fulfill what was spoken through the prophet Isaiah: He took up our infirmities and bore our diseases.*

RSV - *That evening they brought to him many who were possessed with demons; and he cast out the spirits with a word, and healed all who were sick. This was to fulfill what was spoken by the prophet Isaiah, "He took our infirmities and bore our diseases."*

KJV - *When the even was come, they brought unto him many that were possessed with devils: and he cast out the spirits with his word, and healed all that were sick: That it might be fulfilled which was spoken by Esaias the prophet, saying, Himself took our infirmities, and bare our sicknesses.*

LB - *That evening several demon-possessed people were brought to Jesus; and when he spoke a single word, all the demons fled; and all the sick were healed. This fulfilled the prophecy of Isaiah, "He took our sicknesses and bore our diseases."*

NOTE TO THE EDUCATOR

Jesus is a healer. He bore all our iniquities and took on our sicknesses. He has done it all. This is why we are Christ-followers. We believe that He is the All in All and has all power to do all things on our behalf. ALL THINGS! When we have students in our school that are so unruly and even dangerous, Christians call on Jesus because we know that only He can remove evil. We can create programs and devise behavior plans, but only He can unlock the chains that bind and soften hard hearts. We long for a world where everyone calls upon His Name, but in the present we can and will call upon Him on their behalf.

1:16 PM PRAYER

Please pray for the needs of the classroom assistants on our campuses.

QUOTE FOR THE DAY

The difference between ordinary and extraordinary is that little extra. **Unknown**

NOTES:

_____
_____
_____
_____
_____

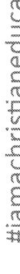

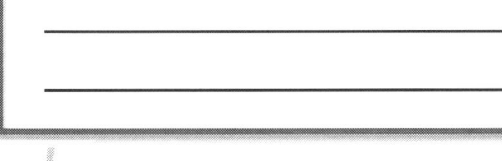
Where we read the Bible with our brother and sisters in the public schools

DAILY PROMISES OF GOD
for educators

MATTHEW 11:28-29

NIV - *Come to me, all you who are weary and burdened, and I will give you rest. Take my yoke upon you and learn from me, for I am gentle and humble in heart, and you will find rest for your souls.*

RSV - *Come to me, all who labor and are heavy laden, and I will give you rest. Take my yoke upon you, and learn from me; for I am gentle and lowly in heart, and you will find rest for your souls.*

KJV - *Come unto me, all ye that labour and are heavy laden, and I will give you rest. Take my yoke upon you, and learn of me; for I am meek and lowly in heart: and ye shall find rest unto your souls.*

LB - *Come to me and I will give you rest—all of you who work so hard beneath a heavy yoke. Wear my yoke—for it fits perfectly—and let me teach you; for I am gentle and humble, and you shall find rest for your souls; for I give you only light burdens.*

NOTE TO THE EDUCATOR

By this time of the year, who wouldn't be tired? Give your burdens to the Lord. He is waiting to give you rest. Why carry a heavy yoke around your neck when His burden is light? He wants to make a great exchange with you. He's such a gentleman. He will never force Himself on you, but He will softly and gently invite you to lift your tired and weary burdens up to Him. There's one hitch. Don't take them back! When the burden is gone and the yoke is lifted, learn to love the freedom and joy of being blessed by His humble spirit. Are you ready for some rest? Let Him teach you for a while.

1:16 PM PRAYER

Please pray for any colleague who is having marital difficulties today.

QUOTE FOR THE DAY

A thorough understanding of the Bible is better than a college education. **Theodore Roosevelt**

NOTES:

_____
_____
_____
_____
_____

DAY 110

#iamachristianeducator

Where we read the Bible with our brother and sisters in the public schools

DAILY PROMISES OF GOD
for educators

MATTHEW 13:43

NIV - *Then the righteous will shine like the sun in the kingdom of their Father. Whoever has ears, let them hear.*

RSV - *Then the righteous will shine like the sun in the kingdom of their Father. He who has ears, let him hear.*

KJV - *Then shall the righteous shine forth as the sun in the kingdom of their Father. Who hath ears to hear, let him hear.*

LB - *Then the godly shall shine as the sun in their Father's Kingdom. Let those with ears, listen!*

NOTE TO THE EDUCATOR

We have such a great hope and promise in our future with our Lord. Let those who have ears, listen! Don't you wish it was that easy in class? Wouldn't it be a great call to action to address our students with, *"You who have ears, listen!"* We can all use some practice listening. Students need to listen to the lessons of their teachers more. Teachers need to listen for the needs of their students better. As colleagues, we need to listen for how we can serve. All in all, listening needs practice. Make it a point today to notice how well you are listening. Begin with yourself to see if you need any practice. Try to form no comebacks when your colleagues are telling their side of a story and see if it's possible to just listen. Listening may be one of the greatest peacemaking tools we can utilize in our school communities.

1:16 PM PRAYER

Please pray to remember to forgive. (Eph. 4:32)

QUOTE FOR THE DAY

Zeal without knowledge is fire without light. **Thomas Henry Huxley**

NOTES:

_____

_____

_____

_____

_____

DAY 111

#iamachristianeducator

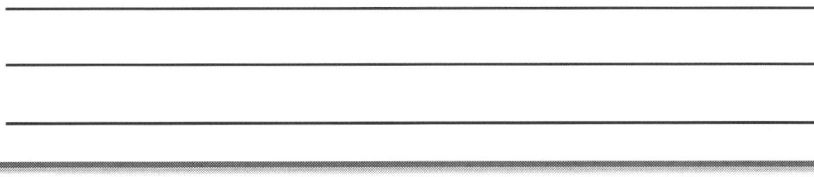
Where we read the Bible with our brother and sisters in the public schools

DAILY PROMISES OF GOD
for educators

MATTHEW 17:20

DAY 112

NIV - He replied, "Because you have so little faith. Truly I tell you, if you have faith as small as a mustard seed, you can say to this mountain, 'Move from here to there,' and it will move. Nothing will be impossible for you."

RSV - He said to them, "Because of your little faith. For truly, I say to you, if you have faith as a grain of mustard seed, you will say to this mountain, 'Move from here to there,' and it will move; and nothing will be impossible to you."

KJV - And Jesus said unto them, Because of your unbelief: for verily I say unto you, If ye have faith as a grain of mustard seed, ye shall say unto this mountain, Remove hence to yonder place; and it shall remove; and nothing shall be impossible unto you.

LB - "Because of your little faith," Jesus told them. "For if you had faith even as small as a tiny mustard seed, you could say to this mountain, 'Move!' and it would go far away. Nothing would be impossible."

NOTE TO THE EDUCATOR

We believe without reservation that God's Truth and Love can transform our public schools. With thousands of Christian educators placed by Him throughout the nation, we have an army of ambassadors who negotiate the systems and customs of public schools which are often foreign to our worldview. We are joined together as the Body of Christ to encourage, equip and empower each other to display the Fruit of the Spirit, to love each other and especially our students. We are called to be the light in dark places and the salt to season and flavor the school environment. Pray big, believe and watch because nothing is impossible with God's help.

1:16 PM PRAYER

Please pray for the needs of our middle school teachers.

QUOTE FOR THE DAY

Don't cry because it's over, smile because it happened. **Unknown**

NOTES:
_____
_____
_____
_____
_____

#iamachristianeducator

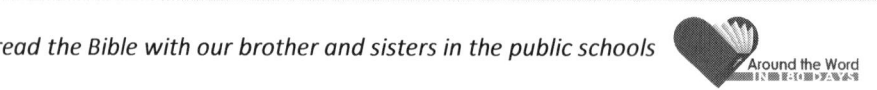

Where we read the Bible with our brother and sisters in the public schools

DAILY PROMISES OF GOD
for educators

MATTHEW 18:19-20

NIV - *Again, truly I tell you that if two of you on earth agree about anything they ask for, it will be done for them by my Father in heaven. For where two or three gather in my name, there am I with them.*

RSV - *Again I say to you, if two of you agree on earth about anything they ask, it will be done for them by my Father in heaven. For where two or three are gathered in my name, there am I in the midst of them."*

KJV - *Again I say unto you, That if two of you shall agree on earth as touching any thing that they shall ask, it shall be done for them of my Father which is in heaven. For where two or three are gathered together in my name, there am I in the midst of them.*

LB - *I also tell you this—if two of you agree down here on earth concerning anything you ask for, my Father in heaven will do it for you. For where two or three gather together because they are mine, I will be right there among them.*

NOTE TO THE EDUCATOR

We are in a great need of prayer groups on our campuses. It is often very difficult to gather your fellow Christian educators because we have to have our prayer time before or after our contract time. It's difficult enough to get to school in time to get the things done for the day. Trying to meet after school is circumvented by meetings, parent conferences or routine interruptions. However, this promise is a call to action! You do not need a large group. You only need two or three to gather and He'll be right there with you. That's unreal! Make every effort to cover your school in prayer often and never worry about only having a small group of people. It only takes two or three to gather and then you have Jesus among you. Wow.

1:16 PM PRAYER

Please pray Psalm 19:14 before we speak.

QUOTE FOR THE DAY

Be who you are and say what you feel, because those who mind don't matter, and those who matter don't mind. **Bernard M. Baruch**

NOTES:

_____

_____

_____

_____

_____

Where we read the Bible with our brother and sisters in the public schools

DAILY PROMISES OF GOD
for educators

MATTHEW 25:34

DAY 114

NIV - *Then the King will say to those on his right, Come, you who are blessed by my Father; take your inheritance, the kingdom prepared for you since the creation of the world.*

RSV - *Then the King will say to those at his right hand, Come, O blessed of my Father, inherit the kingdom prepared for you from the foundation of the world.*

KJV - *Then shall the King say unto them on his right hand, Come, ye blessed of my Father, inherit the kingdom prepared for you from the foundation of the world.*

LB - *Then I, the King, shall say to those at my right, Come, blessed of my Father, into the Kingdom prepared for you from the founding of the world.*

NOTE TO THE EDUCATOR

God has prepared a place for us since the creation of the world. This gives us unbelievable awe. It is our hope and salvation and the reason we desire ALL people to come to Him. In our zeal, we would love to bring the good news to every child, every adult and every human connection in our school life, but we also know that we must be lawful. The 1st Amendment states that *Congress shall make no law establishing a religion nor prohibiting the free exercise thereof…..* We are "Congress" when we are on the clock. We do not proclaim Jesus Christ as Lord and Savior from the front of our classrooms, but we do walk His walk and love those we encounter. We also have the 1st Amendment gift of "*nor prohibiting the free exercise thereof….*" which affords us the legal right to have prayer and Bible study groups with our colleagues. We can also smile as our students have the total right to free expression of their religion as long as they are not interrupting instruction. His kingdom is coming and we yearn for all to come in His timing and in His will.

1:16 PM PRAYER

Please pray for parents to make time to talk about school and be more involved in the learning process.

QUOTE FOR THE DAY

A room without books is like a body without a soul. **Marcus Tullius Cicero**

NOTES:
_____
_____
_____
_____
_____

#iamachristianeducator

Where we read the Bible with our brother and sisters in the public schools

DAILY PROMISES OF GOD
for educators

MARK 9:23

NIV – *"If you can?" said Jesus. "Everything is possible for one who believes."*

RSV - *And Jesus said to him, "If you can! All things are possible to him who believes."*

KJV - *Jesus said unto him, If thou canst believe, all things are possible to him that believeth.*

LB - *"If I can?" Jesus asked. "Anything is possible if you have faith."*

NOTE TO THE EDUCATOR

Everything is possible for one who believes. It sounds like Jesus is setting a challenge for us. Believe and it will be done. Ask and you shall receive. In our world of data driven decisions and standardized everything, it is impossible to measure belief. How do you know if you have enough? Belief is defined as an acceptance that a statement is true or that something exists. It is confidence in someone or something. As Christian educators, we believe that Jesus is our Lord and Savior. We have confidence in His power and ability to carry out His promises. There is no need to wonder if we have a measureable amount of belief, just believe! Take His challenge. When you ask God to help you with school issues, believe and be confident and then stand back and give Him praise when He answers your prayers.

1:16 PM PRAYER

Please pray for the needs of our high school teachers.

QUOTE FOR THE DAY

Be the change that you wish to see in the world. **Mahatma Gandhi**

NOTES:

_____
_____
_____
_____
_____

DAY 115

#iamachristianeducator

Where we read the Bible with our brother and sisters in the public schools

DAILY PROMISES OF GOD
for educators

MARK 11:25

NIV – *And when you stand praying, if you hold anything against anyone, forgive them, so that your Father in heaven may forgive you your sins.*

RSV - *And whenever you stand praying, forgive, if you have anything against any one; so that your Father also who is in heaven may forgive you your trespasses.*

KJV - *And when ye stand praying, forgive, if ye have ought against any: that your Father also which is in heaven may forgive you your trespasses.*

LB - *But when you are praying, first forgive anyone you are holding a grudge against, so that your Father in heaven will forgive you your sins too.*

NOTE TO THE EDUCATOR

A classroom of forgiveness is the mark of a Christian educator. There are many places in the Bible that are "if...then" situations with God. If we do our part, He promises to do His. In this case, how can we expect God to forgive us if we haven't forgiven those who have offended us? At times the offense may come from a colleague, but there are plenty of times an offense comes from our students. How we handle these tense situations is uniquely Christian. We must forgive. It doesn't mean we don't discipline. It does mean that we forgive them their offense so that when we pray, we may stand before God without any offense on our part. Giving students a fresh start each time they enter your classroom is an investment into their learning. It clears the air and gives them a second chance. Our God is a God of second chances. Why not be known as a classroom of second chances?

1:16 PM PRAYER

Please pray for a good rest each night.

QUOTE FOR THE DAY

If you tell the truth, you don't have to remember anything. **Mark Twain**

NOTES:
_____
_____
_____
_____
_____

DAY 116

#iamachristianeducator

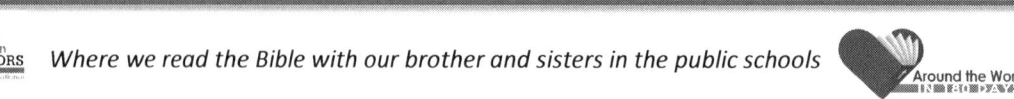
Where we read the Bible with our brother and sisters in the public schools

DAILY PROMISES OF GOD
for educators

LUKE 10:20

DAY 117

NIV – *However, do not rejoice that the spirits submit to you, but rejoice that your names are written in heaven.*

RSV - *Nevertheless do not rejoice in this, that the spirits are subject to you; but rejoice that your names are written in heaven.*

KJV - *Notwithstanding in this rejoice not, that the spirits are subject unto you; but rather rejoice, because your names are written in heaven.*

LB - *However, the important thing is not that demons obey you, but that your names are registered as citizens of heaven.*

NOTE TO THE EDUCATOR

My daughter teaches Algebra 2 Honors and Precalculus and has one of the coolest Hall of Fames in any school. Each year that a student gets all A's on the tests ALL year, their name is entered into the Hall of Fame in her room. Students come back each and every year to see their name hanging on the wall and her new students are encouraged because they know it's possible for them to be on the wall also. We rejoice in a generous God Who has written our names in His book, His Hall of Fame. We are believers who call ourselves Christ-followers because of His unmatched gift of salvation. We don't have to earn straight A's. We don't have to earn anything. We have to believe that He is the One Who did it all. His grace covers us completely. That is why we are Christian educators who seek to grace our students and colleagues with His love knowing that our names are written in heaven.

1:16 PM PRAYER

Please pray to love the unlovable.

QUOTE FOR THE DAY

Insanity is doing the same thing, over and over again, but expecting different results.
Narcotics Anonymous

NOTES:

_____

_____

_____

_____

_____

Where we read the Bible with our brother and sisters in the public schools

#iamachristianeducator

DAILY PROMISES OF GOD
for educators

LUKE 11:13

NIV – *If you then, though you are evil, know how to give good gifts to your children, how much more will your Father in heaven give the Holy Spirit to those who ask him!*

RSV - *If you then, who are evil, know how to give good gifts to your children, how much more will the heavenly Father give the Holy Spirit to those who ask him!*

KJV - *If ye then, being evil, know how to give good gifts unto your children: how much more shall your heavenly Father give the Holy Spirit to them that ask him?*

LB - *And if even sinful persons like yourselves give children what they need, don't you realize that your heavenly Father will do at least as much, and give the Holy Spirit to those who ask for him?*

NOTE TO THE EDUCATOR

We are in the business of giving children what they need. When they need encouragement, we encourage. When they need discipline, we discipline. When they need counsel, we counsel. When they need new skills, we teach. Who encourages the encourager? Who disciplines the one who disciplines? Who counsels the one who counsels? Who teaches the one who teaches? We know that the Holy Spirit is the Counselor, Convicter and Comforter. He is our Advocate and Guide. We need to ask for His help, but we also know that He intercedes on our behalf even when we don't know what to pray. The Holy Spirit indwells all believers which is why it is so important to gather with other Christian educators, that you may all be encouraged. Jesus promised that the Spirit would teach His disciples all things. (John 14:26; 1st Cor. 2:13) Be teachable to be the best educator you can be.

1:16 PM PRAYER

Please pray to display the Fruit of the Spirit - Gal. 5:22-23.

QUOTE FOR THE DAY

A woman is like a tea bag; you never know how strong it is until it's in hot water.
Eleanor Roosevelt

NOTES:
_____
_____
_____
_____
_____

Where we read the Bible with our brother and sisters in the public schools

DAY 118

#iamachristianeducator

DAILY PROMISES OF GOD
for educators

LUKE 12:28-31

NIV – *If that is how God clothes the grass of the field, which is here today, and tomorrow is thrown into the fire, how much more will he clothe you—you of little faith! And do not set your heart on what you will eat or drink; do not worry about it. For the pagan world runs after all such things, and your Father knows that you need them. But seek his kingdom, and these things will be given to you as well.*

RSV - *But if God so clothes the grass which is alive in the field today and tomorrow is thrown into the oven, how much more will he clothe you, O men of little faith! And do not seek what you are to eat and what you are to drink, nor be of anxious mind. For all the nations of the world seek these things; and your Father knows that you need them. Instead, seek his kingdom, and these things shall be yours as well.*

KJV - *If then God so clothe the grass, which is to day in the field, and to morrow is cast into the oven; how much more will he clothe you, O ye of little faith? And seek not ye what ye shall eat, or what ye shall drink, neither be ye of doubtful mind. For all these things do the nations of the world seek after: and your Father knoweth that ye have need of these things. But rather seek ye the kingdom of God; and all these things shall be added unto you.*

LB - *And if God provides clothing for the flowers that are here today and gone tomorrow, don't you suppose that he will provide clothing for you, you doubters? And don't worry about food—what to eat and drink; don't worry at all that God will provide it for you. All mankind scratches for its daily bread, but your heavenly Father knows your needs. He will always give you all you need from day to day if you will make the Kingdom of God your primary concern.*

NOTE TO THE EDUCATOR

I love how the different translations explain our faith (or lack of faith). We who are of anxious mind or you (ye) of little faith or you doubter. We all fear and worry about different things, but as Christian educators, we can step up our game because we are covered. Do we really believe it? When school activities, demands and meetings are overwhelming, sing songs of praise, read the Word and pray. Kingdom seeking is our first priority. It is His promise that He will take care of our needs. Stop trying to do His job!

1:16 PM PRAYER

Please pray for the needs of all elementary teachers.

QUOTE FOR THE DAY

Yesterday is history, tomorrow is a mystery, today is a gift of God, which is why we call it the present. **Bill Keane**

NOTES:

_____

_____

_____

_____

DAY 119

#iamachristianeducator

Where we read the Bible with our brother and sisters in the public schools

DAILY PROMISES OF GOD
for educators

LUKE 12:32

NIV – *Do not be afraid, little flock, for your Father has been pleased to give you the kingdom.*

RSV - *Fear not, little flock, for it is your Father's good pleasure to give you the kingdom.*

KJV - *Fear not, little flock; for it is your Father's good pleasure to give you the kingdom.*

LB - *So don't be afraid, little flock. For it gives your Father great happiness to give you the Kingdom.*

NOTE TO THE EDUCATOR

One of the greatest fears for Christian educators in the public schools is being Christian. We don't always know what we can do or say, or to whom we can share our love. We need not have any fear, dear ones, because our Father is pleased with our kingdom work. Each day that you love on your students and colleagues, you are doing kingdom work. Every time you go out of your way to do acts of kindness and goodness, you are doing kingdom work. You do not have to preach from the mountain tops. Our preaching is our walk. We are different. We are Christians who are to be known by our love. Being holy bold wrapped in love is how to be a legal and graceful Christian in the public schools. If you have specific questions, go to the Christian Educator website, www.ceai.org, and look for **Contact Us**. You can call, write or even search the site for great resources. Continue to love your students and colleagues knowing that you will receive the inheritance from our Lord and Savior Jesus Christ.

1:16 PM PRAYER

Please pray Deuteronomy 31:6 and remember that God is always with us

QUOTE FOR THE DAY

Always forgive your enemies; nothing annoys them as much. **Oscar Wilde**

NOTES:
_____
_____
_____
_____
_____

 Where we read the Bible with our brother and sisters in the public schools

DAILY PROMISES OF GOD
for educators

JOHN 3:16

DAY 121

NIV – *For God so loved the world that he gave his one and only Son, that whoever believes in him shall not perish but have eternal life.*

RSV - *For God so loved the world that he gave his only Son, that whoever believes in him should not perish but have eternal life.*

KJV - *For God so loved the world, that he gave his only begotten Son, that whosoever believeth in him should not perish, but have everlasting life.*

LB - *For God loved the world so much that he gave his only Son so that anyone who believes in him shall not perish but have eternal life.*

NOTE TO THE EDUCATOR

This is one of the most often quoted verses in the whole Bible, particularly at football games. It is the ultimate promise of our belief that Jesus Christ gave His life for us. It is the empowerment of what we do each day. This promise is to all unbelievers also, because when they do believe in Him they too will have eternal life. That is our hope for all our students and colleagues. That is our prayer. When you look into the eyes of your students each day, be reminded that they have or will someday have the same hope as you. Treat them with tender loving care as they grow and develop into the person they were created to be in Him. You may have been given this particular group of students or this particular position for such a time as this.

1:16 PM PRAYER

Please pray for the needs of the school nurse.

QUOTE FOR THE DAY

Of the many influences that have shaped the United States into a distinctive nation and people, none may be said to be more fundamental and enduring than the Bible. **President Ronald Reagan**

NOTES:

_____

_____

_____

_____

_____

#iamachristianeducator

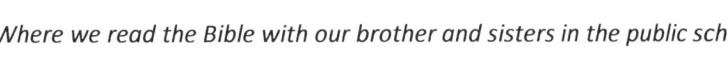
Where we read the Bible with our brother and sisters in the public schools

DAILY PROMISES OF GOD
for educators

JOHN 3:36

NIV – *Whoever believes in the Son has eternal life, but whoever rejects the Son will not see life, for God's wrath remains on them.*

RSV - *He who believes in the Son has eternal life; he who does not obey the Son shall not see life, but the wrath of God rests upon him.*

KJV - *He that believeth on the Son hath everlasting life: and he that believeth not the Son shall not see life; but the wrath of God abideth on him.*

LB - *And all who trust him—God's Son—to save them have eternal life; those who don't believe and obey him shall never see heaven, but the wrath of God remains upon them.*

NOTE TO THE EDUCATOR

Does it break your heart to know that the majority of students and adults in the public schools are unbelievers? Does it motivate you to be the best example of who He is to them? As a public school servant, we cannot lead our students to Christ. We can pray for their salvation, treat them as Jesus would treat them and do purposeful acts of kindness for them. Building up their confidence, sharing their accomplishments and calling home with good news are small ways we can show them Jesus. Try that phone call home for the student who seems discouraged in your classroom. Parents fear the call from the teacher because it is almost always something bad that the student has done. This phone call will be just to let them know that you are so pleased to have their child in your class. This makes a small but powerful connection that they will remember for a long time.

1:16 PM PRAYER

Please pray for creativity and excellence in exercising our gifts.

QUOTE FOR THE DAY

Being deeply loved by someone gives you strength, while loving someone deeply gives you courage. **Lao Tzu**

NOTES:

_____
_____
_____
_____
_____

DAY 122

#iamachristianeducator

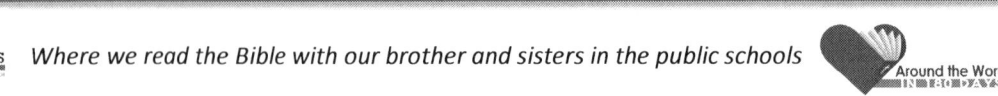

Where we read the Bible with our brother and sisters in the public schools

DAILY PROMISES OF GOD
for educators

JOHN 10:29

NIV – *My Father, who has given them to me, is greater than all; no one can snatch them out of my Father's hand.*

RSV - *My Father, who has given them to me, is greater than all, and no one is able to snatch them out of the Father's hand.*

KJV - *My Father, which gave them me, is greater than all; and no man is able to pluck them out of my Father's hand.*

LB - *For my Father has given them to me, and he is more powerful than anyone else, so no one can kidnap them from me.*

NOTE TO THE EDUCATOR

Have you ever watched a kindergarten teacher in action? They are amazing. I have no idea how they can manage a room full of 5 year-olds (particularly on the first day of school) with the tears, fears and blank stares. It's like herding cats. Yet through the exasperation, you also see calm and courage, grace and love. A kindergarten teacher can get these little students to rotate through centers and even learn to stay on task. They will also guard and protect their little ones at all cost. There is no one on campus who can take their babies away from them. They remind me of our Father's love. Kindergarten students have no fear that anything can happen to them while under the watchful care of their teacher. You have nothing to fear. No one can snatch you away from the Father because you are under the care of Jesus. What a gift.

1:16 PM PRAYER

Please pray for students to learn respect for authority.

QUOTE FOR THE DAY

Women and cats will do as they please, and men and dogs should relax and get used to the idea.
Robert A. Heinlein

NOTES:
___
___
___
___
___

Where we read the Bible with our brother and sisters in the public schools

DAILY PROMISES OF GOD
for educators

JOHN 14:1-3

NIV – *Do not let your hearts be troubled. You believe in God; believe also in me. My Father's house has many rooms; if that were not so, would I have told you that I am going there to prepare a place for you? And if I go and prepare a place for you, I will come back and take you to be with me that you also may be where I am.*

RSV - *Let not your hearts be troubled; believe in God, believe also in me. In my Father's house are many rooms; if it were not so, would I have told you that I go to prepare a place for you? And when I go and prepare a place for you, I will come again and will take you to myself, that where I am you may be also.*

KJV - *Let not your heart be troubled: ye believe in God, believe also in me. In my Father's house are many mansions: if it were not so, I would have told you. I go to prepare a place for you. And if I go and prepare a place for you, I will come again, and receive you unto myself; that where I am, there ye may be also.*

LB - *Let not your heart be troubled. You are trusting God, now trust in me. There are many homes up there where my Father lives, and I am going to prepare them for your coming. When everything is ready, then I will come and get you, so that you can always be with me where I am. If this weren't so, I would tell you plainly.*

NOTE TO THE EDUCATOR

He has prepared a room for us! He is coming back to get us that we may be with Him always! Now if that's not enough to send chills down your spine, I don't know what else could. This is a great Scripture to memorize so that you can pull it up from your heart any time there are obstacles in school. There is no announcement at a faculty meeting that can alter this promise. There is no disaster in our community that can change this promise. There is nothing a student can do to you that can take away this awesome gift. Do not let your heart be troubled, dear educator. We place our hope in this very promise to be His ambassadors that others may know His greatness and that they may have a mansion too!

1:16 PM PRAYER

Please pray that we show God's love today to a co-worker who is hard to love.

QUOTE FOR THE DAY

You may easily be too big for God to use, but never too small. **Dwight L. Moody**

NOTES:
_____
_____
_____
_____
_____

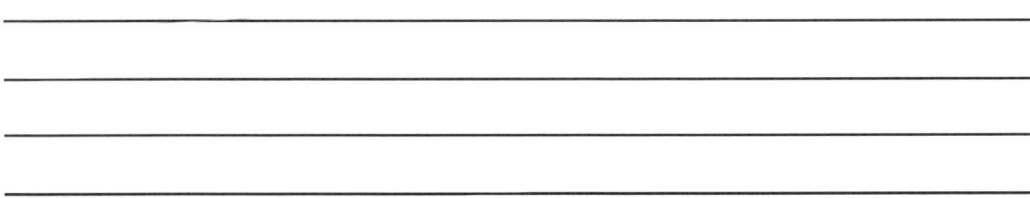

Where we read the Bible with our brother and sisters in the public schools

DAILY PROMISES OF GOD
for educators

JOHN 14:15-16

NIV – *If you love me, keep my commands. And I will ask the Father, and he will give you another advocate to help you and be with you forever.*

RSV - *If you love me, you will keep my commandments. And I will pray the Father, and he will give you another Counselor, to be with you for ever.*

KJV - *If ye love me, keep my commandments. And I will pray the Father, and he shall give you another Comforter, that he may abide with you for ever.*

LB - *If you love me, obey me; and I will ask the Father and he will give you another Comforter, and he will never leave you.*

NOTE TO THE EDUCATOR

The Names of the Holy Spirit include: Comforter, Counselor, Advocate, Guide, Intercessor and Indweller in believers. He is a gift from God through Jesus Christ. The Holy Spirit is advocating for us at all times even when we don't know what to pray for. Think of all the Christians that are on your campus. Some schools are blessed with many believers, both students and educators, who call upon the Lord for help and give praise. In other schools, it seems that you are all alone. I can promise you that you are not. Ask God to help you find a colleague who loves Him. Sometimes, they are simply unaware that they can pray at school and don't realize they have been called to be missionaries. Ask God to help you find a prayer partner who can call upon the Lord with You for the needs of your campus. Praise God for what He will do.

1:16 PM PRAYER

Please pray for the needs of the principal's secretary.

QUOTE FOR THE DAY

If you want your children to be intelligent, read them fairy tales. If you want them to be more intelligent, read them more fairy tales. **Albert Einstein**

NOTES:
_____
_____
_____
_____
_____

Where we read the Bible with our brother and sisters in the public schools

DAILY PROMISES OF GOD
for educators

JOHN 14:27

NIV - *Peace I leave with you; my peace I give you. I do not give to you as the world gives. Do not let your hearts be troubled and do not be afraid.*

RSV - *Peace I leave with you; my peace I give to you; not as the world gives do I give to you. Let not your hearts be troubled, neither let them be afraid.*

KJV - *Peace I leave with you, my peace I give unto you: not as the world giveth, give I unto you. Let not your heart be troubled, neither let it be afraid.*

LB - *I am leaving you with a gift—peace of mind and heart! And the peace I give isn't fragile like the peace the world gives. So don't be troubled or afraid.*

NOTE TO THE EDUCATOR

Our Lord is the Ultimate Gift Giver. Everything that has ever been created has been made by Him. He is the beginning and the end and He has given us the gift of His peace. He has also told us not to be troubled or afraid. Wouldn't it be wonderful to be able to say that to your students? Do not let your hearts be troubled. Do not be afraid. They are only empty words without His authority, but Christian educator, you have Him in you each day you enter the schoolhouse. He can and will help our students with their troubles and fears. Let us pray that they all come to know Him personally. Let these beautiful words of Jesus ring out in your classroom, *"Do not let your hearts be troubled,"* because they are both comforting for your students and recognizable as His words to those who are Christ followers.

1:16 PM PRAYER

Please pray for intentional goodness to everyone you reach out to today.

QUOTE FOR THE DAY

Providence has at all times been my only dependence, for all other resources seem to have failed us. **George Washington**

NOTES:
_____
_____
_____
_____
_____

DAY 126

#iamachristianeducator

Where we read the Bible with our brother and sisters in the public schools

DAILY PROMISES OF GOD
for educators

ACTS 2:38-39

NIV - *Peter replied, "Repent and be baptized, every one of you, in the name of Jesus Christ for the forgiveness of your sins. And you will receive the gift of the Holy Spirit. The promise is for you and your children and for all who are far off—for all whom the Lord our God will call."*

RSV - *And Peter said to them, "Repent, and be baptized every one of you in the name of Jesus Christ for the forgiveness of your sins; and you shall receive the gift of the Holy Spirit. For the promise is to you and to your children and to all that are far off, every one whom the Lord our God calls to him."*

KJV - *Then Peter said unto them, Repent, and be baptized every one of you in the name of Jesus Christ for the remission of sins, and ye shall receive the gift of the Holy Ghost. For the promise is unto you, and to your children, and to all that are afar off, even as many as the Lord our God shall call.*

LB - *And Peter replied, "Each one of you must turn from sin, return to God, and be baptized in the name of Jesus Christ for the forgiveness of your sins; then you also shall receive this gift, the Holy Spirit. For Christ promised him to each one of you who has been called by the Lord our God, and to your children and even to those in distant lands!"*

NOTE TO THE EDUCATOR

The Holy Spirit is a promised gift that God gives us when we repent of our sins and are baptized in the name of Jesus. This is a generational promise. Let us pray today for our own families who have not yet repented and been baptized that they receive this incredible gift. It doesn't matter how far away they are or whether you are estranged or not, but if God has called you, there is not doubt that your yearnings of salvation for your loved ones is great. Look out upon your student population daily and let your heart's cry be for their salvation also. He is a generous God Who is mercy-laden to those who love Him and want to know Him more.

1:16 PM PRAYER

Please pray for gentleness toward everyone we interact with today.

QUOTE FOR THE DAY

All the scholastic scaffolding falls, as a ruined edifice, before one single word....faith.
Napoleon Bonaparte

NOTES:
_____
_____
_____
_____
_____

DAY 127

#iamachristianeducator

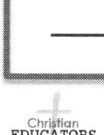
Where we read the Bible with our brother and sisters in the public schools

DAILY PROMISES OF GOD
for educators **ACTS 17:26-28**

DAY 128

NIV - *From one man he made all the nations, that they should inhabit the whole earth; and he marked out their appointed times in history and the boundaries of their lands. God did this so that they would seek him and perhaps reach out for him and find him, though he is not far from any one of us. For in him we live and move and have our being. As some of your own poets have said, We are his offspring.*

RSV - *And he made from one every nation of men to live on all the face of the earth, having determined allotted periods and the boundaries of their habitation, that they should seek God, in the hope that they might feel after him and find him. Yet he is not far from each one of us, for In him we live and move and have our being; as even some of your poets have said, For we are indeed his offspring.*

KJV - *And hath made of one blood all nations of men for to dwell on all the face of the earth, and hath determined the times before appointed, and the bounds of their habitation; that they should seek the Lord, if haply they might feel after him, and find him, though he be not far from every one of us: For in him we live, and move, and have our being; as certain also of your own poets have said, For we are also his offspring.*

LB - *He created all the people of the world from one man, Adam, and scattered the nations across the face of the earth. He decided beforehand which should rise and fall, and when. He determined their boundaries. His purpose in all of this is that they should seek after God, and perhaps feel their way toward him and find him—though he is not far from any one of us. For in him we live and move and are! As one of your own poets says it, We are the sons of God.*

NOTE TO THE EDUCATOR

What a great hope we have for all the students and colleagues, all the people of the world. God has given each of us the purpose of seeking Him and feeling our way towards Him. There is a God-sized hole in each of our hearts that yearns for that connection. Perhaps you may be the only representative of Jesus Christ that your students have ever had. Ask for the wisdom, courage and strength to represent Him well for the future of all our students.

1:16 PM PRAYER

Please pray for wisdom in grading to know when to be firm and when to be merciful.

QUOTE FOR THE DAY

You must undertake something so great that you cannot accomplish it unaided. **Phillip Brooks**

NOTES:

_____
_____
_____
_____

Where we read the Bible with our brother and sisters in the public schools

DAILY PROMISES OF GOD
for educators

ROMANS 6:23

NIV - *For the wages of sin is death, but the gift of God is eternal life in Christ Jesus our Lord.*

RSV - *For the wages of sin is death, but the free gift of God is eternal life in Christ Jesus our Lord.*

KJV - *For the wages of sin is death; but the gift of God is eternal life through Jesus Christ our Lord.*

LB - *For the wages of sin is death, but the free gift of God is eternal life through Jesus Christ our Lord.*

NOTE TO THE EDUCATOR

What does sin look like in the classroom? It's any situation that requires teacher intervention. When a student acts out, we must take care of it. Turning a blind eye to misbehavior or acts of unkindness can condone the behavior. As Christian educators, we can identify misbehavior as sin in our minds because we know that anything that is not done God's way is sinful. When our hearts are pierced to take action against misbehavior, we must act on it. Making an example of one student's wrong doings can save both him/her and any future acts that others may be considering. Ignoring the problem and hoping it goes away, never solves it. Be motived by this awesome gift of eternal life to those of us who know that Jesus Christ our Lord has freely given eternal life to those who love Him.

1:16 PM PRAYER

Please pray for the student who is quiet most of the time.

QUOTE FOR THE DAY

It takes a great deal of bravery to stand up to our enemies, but just as much to stand up to our friends. **J.K. Rowling, Harry Potter and the Sorcerer's Stone**

NOTES:

_____

_____

_____

_____

_____

 Where we read the Bible with our brother and sisters in the public schools

DAILY PROMISES OF GOD
for educators

ROMANS 8:11

NIV - *And if the Spirit of him who raised Jesus from the dead is living in you, he who raised Christ from the dead will also give life to your mortal bodies because of his Spirit who lives in you.*

RSV - *If the Spirit of him who raised Jesus from the dead dwells in you, he who raised Christ Jesus from the dead will give life to your mortal bodies also through his Spirit which dwells in you.*

KJV - *But if the Spirit of him that raised up Jesus from the dead dwell in you, he that raised up Christ from the dead shall also quicken your mortal bodies by his Spirit that dwelleth in you.*

LB - *And if the Spirit of God, who raised up Jesus from the dead, lives in you, he will make your dying bodies live again after you die, by means of this same Holy Spirit living within you.*

NOTE TO THE EDUCATOR

Christians in public education have the Spirit of God living in us and walking our campuses. Christians come in all races, ages, sizes and shapes. Christian educators may include the administrators, bus drivers, custodians, office secretaries and clerks, the teachers, substitutes and coaches. Many of our strongest Christians are the students and they have total religious freedom to bless the school community. Their only barrier is that they may not interrupt instructional time. All of the educators mentioned above can pray privately at any time, corporately before or after contract time and participate in a Bible study if they choose. As long as there are tests in school, there will be prayers. May you pray without ceasing for the needs of your school community.

1:16 PM PRAYER

Please pray to remember that the Word is our guide.

QUOTE FOR THE DAY

The first gift we can bestow on others is a good example. Thomas Morell

NOTES:
_____
_____
_____
_____
_____

DAY 130

 Where we read the Bible with our brother and sisters in the public schools

DAILY PROMISES OF GOD
for educators

ROMANS 8:26

NIV - *In the same way, the Spirit helps us in our weakness. We do not know what we ought to pray for, but the Spirit himself intercedes for us through wordless groans.*

RSV - *Likewise the Spirit helps us in our weakness; for we do not know how to pray as we ought, but the Spirit himself intercedes for us with sighs too deep for words.*

KJV - *Likewise the Spirit also helpeth our infirmities: for we know not what we should pray for as we ought: but the Spirit itself maketh intercession for us with groanings which cannot be uttered.*

LB - *And in the same way—by our faith—the Holy Spirit helps us with our daily problems and in our praying. For we don't even know what we should pray for nor how to pray as we should, but the Holy Spirit prays for us with such feeling that it cannot be expressed in words.*

NOTE TO THE EDUCATOR

When you are not sure what to pray, pray anyway. It is God's promise that the Holy Spirit will be interceding for you with groanings and expressions that we can't even begin to understand. Be postured to pray the moment there is an obstacle on campus. Be ready to pray when students are unruly. Be committed to prayer throughout the school year knowing that the Holy Spirit can ask on our behalf even when we don't know what to ask or how to ask. What a mighty God we serve. I give out pens that have this expression written on them: Prayer – the teacher's greatest tool. It is the reminder that we need to undergird our campuses with the heart of prayer. Let me know if you want me to send you one of those pens!

1:16 PM PRAYER

Please pray to rejoice always and pray without ceasing. (1st Thess. 5:16-17)

QUOTE FOR THE DAY

The gulf between knowledge and truth is infinite. **Henry Miller**

NOTES:

_____

_____

_____

_____

_____

DAY 131

Where we read the Bible with our brother and sisters in the public schools

DAILY PROMISES OF GOD
for educators

ROMANS 8:28

DAY 132

NIV - *And we know that in all things God works for the good of those who love him, who have been called according to his purpose.*

RSV - *We know that in everything God works for good with those who love him, who are called according to his purpose.*

KJV - *And we know that all things work together for good to them that love God, to them who are the called according to his purpose.*

LB - *And we know that all that happens to us is working for our good if we love God and are fitting into his plans.*

NOTE TO THE EDUCATOR

Do you love God? If so, all things will work out this year according to His purpose for you. One thing is for sure, if you are in education and you are listening or reading Around the Word in 180 Days, you have a high calling. God didn't put you at your school for you, but for the others on your campus. Being a blessing to others is part of your high calling. Loving others is your spiritual command. Take steps today to examine yourself to see if you are truly grateful for this high calling even if it's the worst year you have ever had. Serving others and blessing others takes our minds and dedication away from ourselves and on to the mission of being Jesus on our campuses. No words are necessary, just love.

1:16 PM PRAYER

Please pray for God's wisdom to help students deal with anger.

QUOTE FOR THE DAY

Truth is the foundation of all knowledge and the cement of all societies **John Dryden**

NOTES:

_____
_____
_____
_____
_____

#iamachristianeducator

 Where we read the Bible with our brother and sisters in the public schools

DAILY PROMISES OF GOD

for educators

ROMANS 8:31

DAY 133

NIV - *What, then, shall we say in response to these things? If God is for us, who can be against us?*

RSV - *What then shall we say to this? If God is for us, who is against us?*

KJV - *What shall we then say to these things? If God be for us, who can be against us?*

LB - *What can we ever say to such wonderful things as these? If God is on our side, who can ever be against us?*

NOTE TO THE EDUCATOR

God is for us! We are His children. We love Him and serve and call ourselves Christians. What confidence, what joy to be able to say, *"If God is for me, who can be against me?"* The tricky part is believing this awesome promise. The moment you accepted Jesus Christ as your Lord and Savior, you were covered. He really is on your side. There's no room for doubt about that. When an enemy rises against you, repeat this promise as a reminder that He who is in you is greater than the enemy. He will lovingly fight our battles for us. Don't try to take on the enemy alone. There are many enemies in public school that could defeat us, but we serve a mighty God for is for us!

1:16 PM PRAYER

Please pray that we will be merciful and teach our students to be so by example.

QUOTE FOR THE DAY

If a million people believe a foolish thing, it is still a foolish thing. **Anatole France**

NOTES:

_____
_____
_____
_____
_____

#iamachristianeducator

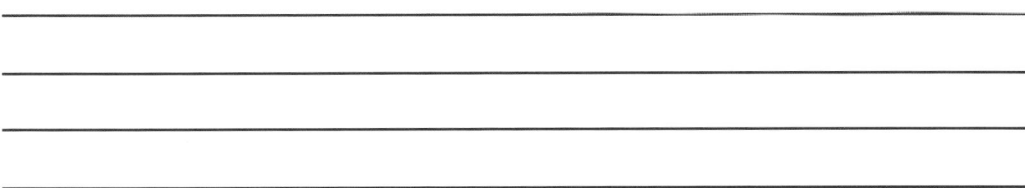

Where we read the Bible with our brother and sisters in the public schools

DAILY PROMISES OF GOD

for educators

ROMANS 8:37-39

NIV - *No, in all these things we are more than conquerors through him who loved us. For I am convinced that neither death nor life, neither angels nor demons, neither the present nor the future, nor any powers, neither height nor depth, nor anything else in all creation, will be able to separate us from the love of God that is in Christ Jesus our Lord.*

RSV - *No, in all these things we are more than conquerors through him who loved us. For I am sure that neither death, nor life, nor angels, nor principalities, nor things present, nor things to come, nor powers, nor height, nor depth, nor anything else in all creation, will be able to separate us from the love of God in Christ Jesus our Lord.*

KJV - *Nay, in all these things we are more than conquerors through him that loved us. For I am persuaded, that neither death, nor life, nor angels, nor principalities, nor powers, nor things present, nor things to come, nor height, nor depth, nor any other creature, shall be able to separate us from the love of God, which is in Christ Jesus our Lord.*

LB - *But despite all this, overwhelming victory is ours through Christ who loved us enough to die for us. For I am convinced that nothing can ever separate us from his love. Death can't, and life can't. The angels won't, and all the powers of hell itself cannot keep God's love away. Our fears for today, our worries about tomorrow, or where we are—high above the sky, or in the deepest ocean—nothing will ever be able to separate us from the love of God demonstrated by our Lord Jesus Christ when he died for us.*

NOTE TO THE EDUCATOR

This is an anchor promise. NOTHING can separate us from the love of God which is in Christ Jesus. No rebellious student, no angry parent, no dissatisfied administrator, no curriculum restraints, no pacing guide, nor any issue that befalls us in the public schools can separate us from our Lord and Savior Jesus Christ. Take courage Christian educator. Hold you head up high. Our King loved us enough to die for us. He is more than able to conqueror any barrier for us.

1:16 PM PRAYER

Please pray for the safety of our students from injury by violence or by accident.

QUOTE FOR THE DAY

Truth is the first chapter in the book of wisdom. **Thomas Jefferson**

NOTES:

_____
_____
_____
_____

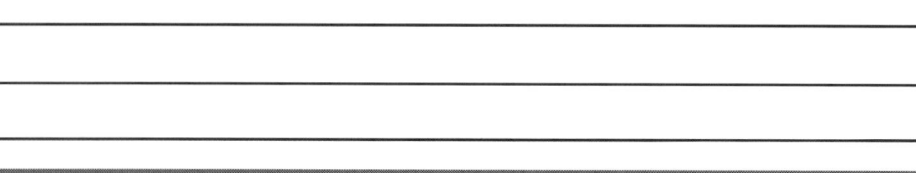

Where we read the Bible with our brother and sisters in the public schools

DAILY PROMISES OF GOD
for educators

ROMANS 10:9

NIV - *If you declare with your mouth, "Jesus is Lord," and believe in your heart that God raised him from the dead, you will be saved.*

RSV - *Because, if you confess with your lips that Jesus is Lord and believe in your heart that God raised him from the dead, you will be saved.*

KJV - *That if thou shalt confess with thy mouth the Lord Jesus, and shalt believe in thine heart that God hath raised him from the dead, thou shalt be saved.*

LB - *For if you tell others with your own mouth that Jesus Christ is your Lord and believe in your own heart that God has raised him from the dead, you will be saved.*

NOTE TO THE EDUCATOR

This is the Gospel promise, the promise of all promises. We are saved by confessing that Jesus is Lord. We need to say it with our own mouth, believe in our heart and know that Jesus was raised from the dead and then it is God's promise that we will have eternal life. Have you done that? If you haven't ever said it aloud, let's do it now. Use your own words but feel free to use this simple prayer. There's no magic, just belief.

Dear Lord, I confess right now that I am a sinner and I need You. I believe that You died for me and then were raised from the dead that I may live eternally with You. Lord, please save me. I understand that it is nothing that I do, but that I am saved by what you have done. I love you Lord, Amen.

1:16 PM PRAYER

Please pray for endurance in the difficult moments

QUOTE FOR THE DAY

Setting a good example is not the main means of influencing others, it is the only means.
Albert Einstein

NOTES:

_____
_____
_____
_____
_____

Where we read the Bible with our brother and sisters in the public schools

DAILY PROMISES OF GOD
for educators

1ST CORINTHIANS 1:4-7

NIV - *I always thank my God for you because of his grace given you in Christ Jesus. For in him you have been enriched in every way—with all kinds of speech and with all knowledge— God thus confirming our testimony about Christ among you. Therefore you do not lack any spiritual gift as you eagerly wait for our Lord Jesus Christ to be revealed.*

RSV - *I give thanks to God always for you because of the grace of God which was given you in Christ Jesus, that in every way you were enriched in him with all speech and all knowledge— even as the testimony to Christ was confirmed among you— so that you are not lacking in any spiritual gift, as you wait for the revealing of our Lord Jesus Christ;*

KJV - *I thank my God always on your behalf, for the grace of God which is given you by Jesus Christ; That in every thing ye are enriched by him, in all utterance, and in all knowledge; Even as the testimony of Christ was confirmed in you: So that ye come behind in no gift; waiting for the coming of our Lord Jesus Christ:*

LB - *I can never stop thanking God for all the wonderful gifts he has given you, now that you are Christ's: he has enriched your whole life. He has helped you speak out for him and has given you a full understanding of the truth; what I told you Christ could do for you has happened! Now you have every grace and blessing; every spiritual gift and power for doing his will are yours during this time of waiting for the return of our Lord Jesus Christ.*

NOTE TO THE EDUCATOR

I feel like Paul. I thank God for you, Christian educator, every day. I thank God that our students have Christians leading them, guiding them, praying for them and gently teaching them all they need. I thank God for your high calling. I thank God that you have accepted Jesus Christ as your Lord and Savior and that you can walk in His purposes. I am grateful that you join us in Around the Word in 180 days to stay ground in His promises and prayer. All gifts and power are from Him and are His will for you to succeed.

1:16 PM PRAYER

Please pray for teachers and assistants who serve special needs students.

QUOTE FOR THE DAY

The quality of a person's life is in direct proportion to their commitment to excellence, regardless of their chosen field of endeavor. **Vince Lombardi**

NOTES:
_____
_____
_____
_____

DAY 136

#iamachristianeducator

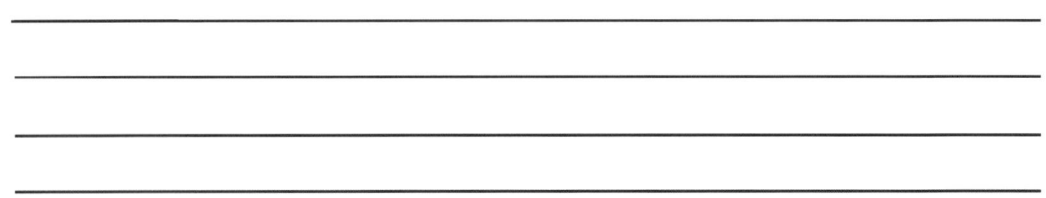
Where we read the Bible with our brother and sisters in the public schools

DAILY PROMISES OF GOD
for educators

1ST CORINTHIANS 2:9

NIV - *However, as it is written: What no eye has seen, what no ear has heard, and what no human mind has conceived — the things God has prepared for those who love him.*

RSV - *But, as it is written, What no eye has seen, nor ear heard, nor the heart of man conceived, what God has prepared for those who love him.*

KJV - *But as it is written, Eye hath not seen, nor ear heard, neither have entered into the heart of man, the things which God hath prepared for them that love him.*

LB - *That is what is meant by the Scriptures which say that no mere man has ever seen, heard, or even imagined what wonderful things God has ready for those who love the Lord.*

NOTE TO THE EDUCATOR

The song by Mercy Me comes to mind while reading this promise, "I Can Only Imagine." God's ways are so much higher than ours and His thoughts are so much greater than ours. How can we possibly know what He has in store for His believers. Trying to imagine God's fulfillment of His promise will put a big smile on your face. As you walk down the hall, try to imagine God's wondrous ways and as you are walking and pondering, don't be surprised if others wonder what you are thinking about with the big grin on your face. To God be the Glory.

1:16 PM PRAYER

Please pray that we will be able to bear, believe, hope and endure all things. (1st Cor. 13:7)

QUOTE FOR THE DAY

The person has achieved success who has loved much, laughed often and been an inspiration to children. **Author Unknown**

NOTES:
_____
_____
_____
_____
_____

DAY 137

#iamachristianeducator

Where we read the Bible with our brother and sisters in the public schools

DAILY PROMISES OF GOD
for educators

1ST CORINTHIANS 10:13

NIV - *No temptation has overtaken you except what is common to mankind. And God is faithful; he will not let you be tempted beyond what you can bear. But when you are tempted, he will also provide a way out so that you can endure it.*

RSV - *No temptation has overtaken you that is not common to man. God is faithful, and he will not let you be tempted beyond your strength, but with the temptation will also provide the way of escape, that you may be able to endure it.*

KJV - *There hath no temptation taken you but such as is common to man: but God is faithful, who will not suffer you to be tempted above that ye are able; but will with the temptation also make a way to escape, that ye may be able to bear it.*

LB - *But remember this—the wrong desires that come into your life aren't anything new and different. Many others have faced exactly the same problems before you. And no temptation is irresistible. You can trust God to keep the temptation from becoming so strong that you can't stand up against it, for he has promised this and will do what he says. He will show you how to escape temptation's power so that you can bear up patiently against it.*

NOTE TO THE EDUCATOR

What is your biggest pressure at school? Who is the person that seems to be able to get to you every time? Why can't you seem to be able to go home without lugging endless things to do only to leave the bag at the door untouched until the next day? These are God-sized problems. Ask and believe that He will help you because He has promised to show a way of escape so that you can endure anything. This promise is like a gift that is never unwrapped. Go for it, tear off the wrapping and claim this promise.

1:16 PM PRAYER

Please pray that we may be a blessing to God rather than asking Him to bless us.

QUOTE FOR THE DAY

We are each of us angels with only one wing. And we can only fly embracing each other.
Luciano De Creshenzo

NOTES:
_____
_____
_____
_____

DAY 138

#iamachristianeducator

  Where we read the Bible with our brother and sisters in the public schools

DAILY PROMISES OF GOD
for educators

2ND CORINTHIANS 1:20-22

NIV - *For no matter how many promises God has made, they are "Yes" in Christ. And so through him the "Amen" is spoken by us to the glory of God. Now it is God who makes both us and you stand firm in Christ. He anointed us, set his seal of ownership on us, and put his Spirit in our hearts as a deposit, guaranteeing what is to come.*

RSV - *For all the promises of God find their Yes in him. That is why we utter the Amen through him, to the glory of God. But it is God who establishes us with you in Christ, and has commissioned us; he has put his seal upon us and given us his Spirit in our hearts as a guarantee.*

KJV - *For all the promises of God in him are yea, and in him Amen, unto the glory of God by us. Now he which stablisheth us with you in Christ, and hath anointed us, is God; Who hath also sealed us, and given the earnest of the Spirit in our hearts.*

LB - *He carries out and fulfills all of God's promises, no matter how many of them there are; and we have told everyone how faithful he is, giving glory to his name. It is this God who has made you and me into faithful Christians and commissioned us apostles to preach the Good News. He has put his brand upon us—his mark of ownership—and given us his Holy Spirit in our hearts as guarantee that we belong to him and as the first installment of all that he is going to give us.*

NOTE TO THE EDUCATOR

You are commissioned to be His faithful servant in the field of public education. I can't think of any higher calling. Every time we say, "Amen" in prayer we are in agreement with Him Who had promised us eternal life. Your calling as an educator is merely a first installment of His riches that He will bestow upon you. What a great company of saints we are together to touch the next generation with His Love and Truth. May you teach like Jesus every day.

1:16 PM PRAYER

Please pray that we are able to help our students realize their God-given potential.

QUOTE FOR THE DAY

We cannot live only for ourselves. A thousand fibers connect us with our fellow men!
Herman Melville

NOTES:

_____

_____

_____

_____

_____

Where we read the Bible with our brother and sisters in the public schools

DAILY PROMISES OF GOD
for educators

2ND CORINTHIANS 5:1

DAY 140

NIV - *For we know that if the earthly tent we live in is destroyed, we have a building from God, an eternal house in heaven, not built by human hands.*

RSV - *For we know that if the earthly tent we live in is destroyed, we have a building from God, a house not made with hands, eternal in the heavens.*

KJV - *For we know that if our earthly house of this tabernacle were dissolved, we have a building of God, an house not made with hands, eternal in the heavens.*

LB - *For we know that when this tent we live in now is taken down—when we die and leave these bodies—we will have wonderful new bodies in heaven, homes that will be ours forevermore, made for us by God himself and not by human hands.*

NOTE TO THE EDUCATOR

Is there anything more difficult to deal with in school than the death of a student or colleague? It rocks the whole campus. In these times, Christians take heart because we believe this glorious promise. He is going to give us a new body that He has made that will be incorruptible and perfect. When non-believers die, it's so much harder. Where is their hope? Let us pray diligently for the salvation of those we interact with each day on our school campus that they too will know and treasure the great promises of our Lord.

1:16 PM PRAYER

Please pray for sharp, Godly young people to become teacher-servants in this great mission field.

QUOTE FOR THE DAY

Four steps to achievement: plan purposefully, prepare prayerfully, proceed positively and pursue persistently. **William Ward**

NOTES:
_____
_____
_____
_____
_____

#iamachristianeducator

Where we read the Bible with our brother and sisters in the public schools

DAILY PROMISES OF GOD
for educators

2ND CORINTHIANS 5:17

DAY 141

NIV - *Therefore, if anyone is in Christ, the new creation has come: The old has gone, the new is here!*

RSV - *Therefore, if any one is in Christ, he is a new creation; the old has passed away, behold, the new has come.*

KJV - *Therefore if any man be in Christ, he is a new creature: old things are passed away; behold, all things are become new.*

LB - *When someone becomes a Christian, he becomes a brand new person inside. He is not the same anymore. A new life has begun!*

NOTE TO THE EDUCATOR

By this time of the school year we can become jaded, stale or ho-hum. Look inside Christian educator. You are new. You have a new life in Christ Jesus. All things are fresh and renewable. Call on Him today to do what He is absolutely best at – regeneration. Are your lessons showing signs of routine? Ask Him to revitalize them. Ask Him to show you how to engage your students. Are your conversations more negative than positive? Ask Him to give you eyes to see and ears to hear what others need. Invite the Creator Himself into your classroom. He's there with you each day. Don't get in His way. Let Him be the lead.

1:16 PM PRAYER

Please pray for our administrators to make wise decisions concerning next year's plans.

QUOTE FOR THE DAY

Children need models more than they need critics. **J. Joubert**

NOTES:
_____
_____
_____
_____
_____

#iamachristianeducator

Where we read the Bible with our brother and sisters in the public schools

DAILY PROMISES OF GOD
for educators

2ND CORINTHIANS 12:9

DAY 1442

NIV - *But he said to me, "My grace is sufficient for you, for my power is made perfect in weakness." Therefore I will boast all the more gladly about my weaknesses, so that Christ's power may rest on me.*

RSV - *But he said to me, "My grace is sufficient for you, for my power is made perfect in weakness." I will all the more gladly boast of my weaknesses, that the power of Christ may rest upon me.*

KJV - *And he said unto me, My grace is sufficient for thee: for my strength is made perfect in weakness. Most gladly therefore will I rather glory in my infirmities, that the power of Christ may rest upon me.*

LB - *Each time he said, "No. But I am with you; that is all you need. My power shows up best in weak people." Now I am glad to boast about how weak I am; I am glad to be a living demonstration of Christ's power, instead of showing off my own power and abilities.*

NOTE TO THE EDUCATOR

It's hard to admit to weakness, yet as a Christian educator we know that Christ works best when we are weak because He is strong. What are your weak spots this year? What has you most frustrated? What are the toughest things to tackle? Find a trusted Christian colleague that you can talk to about this because when we confess our sins, He is right and just to forgive us and cleanse us from all unrighteousness. If you are uncomfortable confessing to a colleague, confess to Him because His grace is sufficient for <u>all</u> your trials.

1:16 PM PRAYER

Please pray for the student who talks too much.

QUOTE FOR THE DAY

Small kindnesses, small courtesies, small considerations, give a greater charm to the character than the display of great talents and accomplishments. **Mary Ann Kelty**

NOTES:
_____
_____
_____
_____
_____

#iamachristianeducator

 Where we read the Bible with our brother and sisters in the public schools

DAILY PROMISES OF GOD
for educators

GALATIANS 3:29

NIV - *If you belong to Christ, then you are Abraham's seed, and heirs according to the promise.*

RSV - *And if you are Christ's, then you are Abraham's offspring, heirs according to promise.*

KJV - *And if ye be Christ's, then are ye Abraham's seed, and heirs according to the promise.*

LB - *And now that we are Christ's we are the true descendants of Abraham, and all of God's promises to him belong to us.*

NOTE TO THE EDUCATOR

Dearest believer,
We are true descendants of Abraham in Christ. Do you remember what God promised Abraham, the father of the faith? He promised that he would become a great nation and a great name, that He would bless those who blessed him and would curse those who cursed him and that in Abraham eventually ALL nations will be blessed. As a seed, we are heirs of these promises and it is through the gift of our high calling that we may bless our students and colleagues. Let the light of Jesus Christ shine through you to bless all your human connections today.
Your sister,
K

1:16 PM PRAYER

Please pray to remember that God has promised us a future and a hope.

QUOTE FOR THE DAY

True education doesn't merely bring us learning, but love of learning; not merely work, but love of work. **Author Unknown**

NOTES:

_____
_____
_____
_____
_____

Where we read the Bible with our brother and sisters in the public schools

DAILY PROMISES OF GOD
for educators

GALATIANS 4:6-7

NIV - *Because you are his sons, God sent the Spirit of his Son into our hearts, the Spirit who calls out, "Abba, Father." So you are no longer a slave, but God's child; and since you are his child, God has made you also an heir.*

RSV - *And because you are sons, God has sent the Spirit of his Son into our hearts, crying, "Abba! Father!" So through God you are no longer a slave but a son, and if a son then an heir.*

KJV - *And because ye are sons, God hath sent forth the Spirit of his Son into your hearts, crying, Abba, Father. Wherefore thou art no more a servant, but a son; and if a son, then an heir of God through Christ.*

LB - *And because we are his sons, God has sent the Spirit of his Son into our hearts, so now we can rightly speak of God as our dear Father. Now we are no longer slaves but God's own sons. And since we are his sons, everything he has belongs to us, for that is the way God planned.*

NOTE TO THE EDUCATOR

Have you ever seen the picture of John-John, President Kennedy's son, hiding under his desk in the Oval Office? No matter what was going on, his young son has access to crawl up into his father's lap. Our God, Our Father is so much more generous, loving and tender-hearted than any human father. We can crawl right up into His lap anytime we need His comfort, advise or love. When we accepted His Son Jesus Christ as our Lord and Savior, we were adopted into the family and can call Him Abba Father. We are now an heir of the promise. May you call on Abba today for all the needs of your school community.

1:16 PM PRAYER

Please pray for the needs of those students who are also parents themselves.

QUOTE FOR THE DAY

The task of the modern educator is not to cut down jungles, but to irrigate deserts. **C.S. Lewis**

NOTES:
_____
_____
_____
_____
_____

DAY 144

#iamachristianeducator

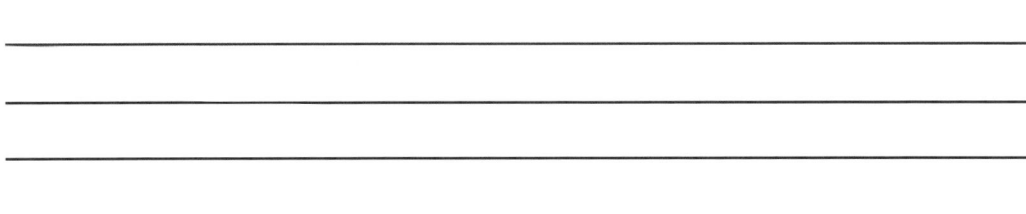

Where we read the Bible with our brother and sisters in the public schools

DAILY PROMISES OF GOD
for educators

GALATIANS 6:9

NIV - *Let us not become weary in doing good, for at the proper time we will reap a harvest if we do not give up.*

RSV - *And let us not grow weary in well-doing, for in due season we shall reap, if we do not lose heart.*

KJV - *And let us not be weary in well doing: for in due season we shall reap, if we faint not.*

LB - *And let us not get tired of doing what is right, for after a while we will reap a harvest of blessing if we don't get discouraged and give up.*

NOTE TO THE EDUCATOR

Doing the right thing is always right. Don't grow weary, dear friend. Continue to sow seeds of goodness, kindness and gentleness into your students. Don't give up on the students who have seemed to tune out. Feed into them with love, mercy and grace. Doing the right thing for us as Christians means doing things as Jesus would do them. He went to the downtrodden, to the hungry and poor. We can't give up on them and even if we don't see any progress now, someday your labor in the Lord will be rewarded. What a promise.

1:16 PM PRAYER

Please pray for extra sensitivity.

QUOTE FOR THE DAY

Education is not the filling of a pail, but the lighting of a fire. **William Butler Yeats**

NOTES:

_____
_____
_____
_____
_____

Where we read the Bible with our brother and sisters in the public schools

DAILY PROMISES OF GOD
for educators

EPHESIANS 1:13-14

NIV - *And you also were included in Christ when you heard the message of truth, the gospel of your salvation. When you believed, you were marked in him with a seal, the promised Holy Spirit, who is a deposit guaranteeing our inheritance until the redemption of those who are God's possession—to the praise of his glory.*

RSV - *In him you also, who have heard the word of truth, the gospel of your salvation, and have believed in him, were sealed with the promised Holy Spirit, which is the guarantee of our inheritance until we acquire possession of it, to the praise of his glory.*

KJV - *In whom ye also trusted, after that ye heard the word of truth, the gospel of your salvation: in whom also after that ye believed, ye were sealed with that holy Spirit of promise, Which is the earnest of our inheritance until the redemption of the purchased possession, unto the praise of his glory.*

LB - *And because of what Christ did, all you others too, who heard the Good News about how to be saved, and trusted Christ, were marked as belonging to Christ by the Holy Spirit, who long ago had been promised to all of us Christians. His presence within us is God's guarantee that he really will give us all that he promised; and the Spirit's seal upon us means that God has already purchased us and that he guarantees to bring us to himself. This is just one more reason for us to praise our glorious God.*

NOTE TO THE EDUCATOR

Did you ever think of yourself as being sealed with the promised Holy Spirit? It is the guarantee or our inheritance. We believe because He is a God of the Ultimate Promise of eternal life. Take heart Christian educator. You are sign, sealed and delivered. You are purchased, promised and provided for. Look at today through the lens of eternity. Look at each of those students you serve to see His image. Look today at your colleagues and treasure them as His. Pray for them all that they too someday will know Him as we do and become part of the great family of God.

1:16 PM PRAYER

Please pray that we show God's love to the student that is hard to love.

QUOTE FOR THE DAY

Too often we give our children answers to remember rather than problems to solve. **Roger Lewin**

NOTES:
_____
_____
_____
_____
_____

DAY 146

#iamachristianeducator

Where we read the Bible with our brother and sisters in the public schools

DAILY PROMISES OF GOD
for educators

EPHESIANS 2:4-7

NIV - *But because of his great love for us, God, who is rich in mercy, made us alive with Christ even when we were dead in transgressions—it is by grace you have been saved. And God raised us up with Christ and seated us with him in the heavenly realms in Christ Jesus, in order that in the coming ages he might show the incomparable riches of his grace, expressed in his kindness to us in Christ Jesus.*

RSV - *But God, who is rich in mercy, out of the great love with which he loved us, even when we were dead through our trespasses, made us alive together with Christ (by grace you have been saved), and raised us up with him, and made us sit with him in the heavenly places in Christ Jesus, that in the coming ages he might show the immeasurable riches of his grace in kindness toward us in Christ Jesus.*

KJV - *But God, who is rich in mercy, for his great love wherewith he loved us, Even when we were dead in sins, hath quickened us together with Christ, (by grace ye are saved;) And hath raised us up together, and made us sit together in heavenly places in Christ Jesus: That in the ages to come he might shew the exceeding riches of his grace in his kindness toward us through Christ Jesus.*

LB - *But God is so rich in mercy; he loved us so much that even though we were spiritually dead and doomed by our sins, he gave us back our lives again when he raised Christ from the dead—only by his undeserved favor have we ever been saved— and lifted us up from the grave into glory along with Christ, where we sit with him in the heavenly realms—all because of what Christ Jesus did. And now God can always point to us as examples of how very, very rich his kindness is, as shown in all he has done for us through Jesus Christ.*

NOTE TO THE EDUCATOR

We are always looking for good examples for students to emulate. They often turn to Hollywood or major sports teams, but Christ followers are the examples that God points to show the richness of Christ's love. IT IS BY GRACE THAT YOU HAVE BEEN SAVED. He did everything, we did nothing to deserve such a future. We are examples of amazing grace for we once we were lost and now we are found.

1:16 PM PRAYER

Please pray that lessons taught today will meet the needs of the students.

QUOTE FOR THE DAY

Treat people as if they were what they ought to be and you help them to become what they are capable of being. - **Goethe**

NOTES:

_____

_____

_____

_____

DAY 147

#iamachristianeducator

Where we read the Bible with our brother and sisters in the public schools

DAILY PROMISES OF GOD
for educators

EPHESIANS 3:6

NIV - *This mystery is that through the gospel the Gentiles are heirs together with Israel, members together of one body, and sharers together in the promise in Christ Jesus.*

RSV - *That is, how the Gentiles are fellow heirs, members of the same body, and partakers of the promise in Christ Jesus through the gospel.*

KJV - *That the Gentiles should be fellowheirs, and of the same body, and partakers of his promise in Christ by the gospel:*

LB - *And this is the secret: that the Gentiles will have their full share with the Jews in all the riches inherited by God's sons; both are invited to belong to his Church, and all of God's promises of mighty blessings through Christ apply to them both when they accept the Good News about Christ and what he has done for them.*

NOTE TO THE EDUCATOR

Aren't you glad we serve a God Who is no respecter of persons? All are invited to share in the promises through Christ Jesus and we long for the day when every eye will see, every knee will bend, every head will bow and and every tongue will confess that Jesus is Lord. Every nation, every language, every race and every creed will bow to King Jesus. Our public schools in America are a microcosm of the whole nation. We serve students of every race, every creed, every tongue and every disposition. Let us not be a respecter of persons and see each and every student with eternal potential.

1:16 PM PRAYER

Please pray for the educators who have sick children at home.

QUOTE FOR THE DAY

The really great teacher is the teacher who makes every student feel great. **G.K. Chesterton**

NOTES:

_____

_____

_____

_____

_____

Where we read the Bible with our brother and sisters in the public schools

DAILY PROMISES OF GOD
for educators

EPHESIANS 3:12

NIV - *In him and through faith in him we may approach God with freedom and confidence.*

RSV - *In whom we have boldness and confidence of access through our faith in him.*

KJV - *In whom we have boldness and access with confidence by the faith of him.*

LB - *Now we can come fearlessly right into God's presence, assured of his glad welcome when we come with Christ and trust in him.*

NOTE TO THE EDUCATOR

If you look at all four of these verses and combine the description of how we can approach God it is amazing. We can come to Him with freedom. We can come to Him with confidence. We can come fearlessly and with boldness. We only have this great ability because of our trust in Christ Jesus. Let us pray, Christian educator, with our whole heart for the needs of our students. Let us pray for all our support team: the custodians, secretaries, coaches, bus drivers, substitutes, crossing guards and assistants. Let us pray for our administrators, school board members and superintendents. Let us pray fearlessly with boldness.

1:16 PM PRAYER

Please pray for Christian brothers and sisters to know they are not alone.

QUOTE FOR THE DAY

Encouragement is the oxygen of the soul. **Author Unknown**

NOTES:
_____
_____
_____
_____
_____

Where we read the Bible with our brother and sisters in the public schools

DAY 149

#iamachristianeducator

DAILY PROMISES OF GOD
for educators

EPHESIANS 3:17-19

NIV - *...so that Christ may dwell in your hearts through faith. And I pray that you, being rooted and established in love, may have power, together with all the Lord's holy people, to grasp how wide and long and high and deep is the love of Christ, and to know this love that surpasses knowledge—that you may be filled to the measure of all the fullness of God.*

RSV - *...and that Christ may dwell in your hearts through faith; that you, being rooted and grounded in love, may have power to comprehend with all the saints what is the breadth and length and height and depth, and to know the love of Christ which surpasses knowledge, that you may be filled with all the fulness of God.*

KJV - *That Christ may dwell in your hearts by faith; that ye, being rooted and grounded in love, May be able to comprehend with all saints what is the breadth, and length, and depth, and height; And to know the love of Christ, which passeth knowledge, that ye might be filled with all the fulness of God.*

LB - *And I pray that Christ will be more and more at home in your hearts, living within you as you trust in him. May your roots go down deep into the soil of God's marvelous love; and may you be able to feel and understand, as all God's children should, how long, how wide, how deep, and how high his love really is; and to experience this love for yourselves, though it is so great that you will never see the end of it or fully know or understand it. And so at last you will be filled up with God himself.*

NOTE TO THE EDUCATOR

In education, we live in the world of knowledge, however, we also live in the tension of trying to understanding the knowledge of Christ's love. How can we possibly grasp the height and depth, the width and length of His love. It is an experience that surpasses knowledge. When we teach our lessons, let us humbly recognize that what we teach today may not even be remembered, but how we treat our students will have a lasting effect. Let us show the love of Christ in all that we do for it will surpass all knowledge.

1:16 PM PRAYER

Please pray that Spring Break (whenever you have it) is refreshing for teachers and students.

QUOTE FOR THE DAY

I praise loudly. I blame softly. **Catherine II of Russia**

NOTES:

_____
_____
_____
_____
_____

DAY 150

#iamachristianeducator

Where we read the Bible with our brother and sisters in the public schools

DAILY PROMISES OF GOD
for educators

EPHESIANS 6:9

NIV - *And masters, treat your slaves in the same way. Do not threaten them, since you know that he who is both their Master and yours is in heaven, and there is no favoritism with him.*

RSV - *Masters, do the same to them, and forbear threatening, knowing that he who is both their Master and yours is in heaven, and that there is no partiality with him.*

KJV - *And, ye masters, do the same things unto them, forbearing threatening: knowing that your Master also is in heaven; neither is there respect of persons with him.*

LB - *And you slave owners must treat your slaves right, just as I have told them to treat you. Don't keep threatening them; remember, you yourselves are slaves to Christ; you have the same Master they do, and he has no favorites.*

NOTE TO THE EDUCATOR

You can catch more flies with honey than with vinegar. Our classroom environments need to be inviting and safe. As the "master" of our classrooms or offices, the way we treat our students and colleagues has an accountability clause. We all have the same Master to answer to and His promise is that He has no favorites. Praise the Lord for that. Let us make a conscious effort to examine ourselves and see if we have favoritism in our interactions with our students. Throw out a wider net of kindness to include all your students with intention. How do you know if you are showing partiality? Be brave and ask one of your students. Out of the mouth of babes will come the truth.

1:16 PM PRAYER

Please pray to show the love of Christ to others because He loved us first.

QUOTE FOR THE DAY

To endure is the first thing that a child ought to learn, and that which he will have the most need to know. **Jean Jacques Rousseau**

NOTES:
_____
_____
_____
_____
_____

DAY 151

#iamachristianeducator

 Where we read the Bible with our brother and sisters in the public schools

DAILY PROMISES OF GOD
for educators

EPHESIANS 6:10-11

NIV - *Finally, be strong in the Lord and in his mighty power. Put on the full armor of God, so that you can take your stand against the devil's schemes.*

RSV - *Finally, be strong in the Lord and in the strength of his might. Put on the whole armor of God, that you may be able to stand against the wiles of the devil.*

KJV - *Finally, my brethren, be strong in the Lord, and in the power of his might. Put on the whole armour of God, that ye may be able to stand against the wiles of the devil.*

LB - *Last of all I want to remind you that your strength must come from the Lord's mighty power within you. Put on all of God's armor so that you will be able to stand safe against all strategies and tricks of Satan.*

NOTE TO THE EDUCATOR

Reminder. Reminder. Your strength comes from the mighty Lord within you. Don't leave for the day without being fully dressed. Put on the helmet of salvation as the reminder of His ultimate promise. Add the belt of truth around your waist and the breast plate of righteousness across your chest. Wear shoes that will remind you of the peace of God and how you represent Him in your walk. You will need your shield of faith to guard you and the sword of the Spirit which is the Word of God. Once you are fully dressed, pray continually. Ask for anything in line with God's will and take your stand as a soldier of Christ.

1:16 PM PRAYER

Please pray for the needs of our testing coordinators

QUOTE FOR THE DAY

If you are swept off your feet, it's time to get on your knees. **Fred Beck**

NOTES:
_____
_____
_____
_____
_____

Where we read the Bible with our brother and sisters in the public schools

DAILY PROMISES OF GOD
for educators

PHILIPPIANS 1:4-6

NIV - *In all my prayers for all of you, I always pray with joy because of your partnership in the gospel from the first day until now, being confident of this, that he who began a good work in you will carry it on to completion until the day of Christ Jesus.*

RSV - *...always in every prayer of mine for you all making my prayer with joy, thankful for your partnership in the gospel from the first day until now. And I am sure that he who began a good work in you will bring it to completion at the day of Jesus Christ.*

KJV - *Always in every prayer of mine for you all making request with joy, For your fellowship in the gospel from the first day until now; Being confident of this very thing, that he which hath begun a good work in you will perform it until the day of Jesus Christ:*

LB - *When I pray for you, my heart is full of joy because of all your wonderful help in making known the Good News about Christ from the time you first heard it until now. And I am sure that God who began the good work within you will keep right on helping you grow in his grace until his task within you is finally finished on that day when Jesus Christ returns.*

NOTE TO THE EDUCATOR

Everything Christ does for us and in us points to His return. I love this encouragement from Paul because not only does he set the example of praying for us, he can say with confidence that He Who began a good work in you will see it through to completion. Your high calling is no accident. You can not effectively remain in education without big picture thinking. Christian educators have a great advantage because we know that we are working for the Lord and that He will not only see us through, but holds the inheritance as our reward. Let us give thanks and pray for the needs of others as we remain confident in Him.

1:16 PM PRAYER

Please pray that we may be peacemakers among our colleagues.

QUOTE FOR THE DAY

Prayer is not conquering God's reluctance, but taking hold of God's willingness. **Phillip Brooks**

NOTES:

_____
_____
_____
_____
_____

Where we read the Bible with our brother and sisters in the public schools

DAILY PROMISES OF GOD
for educators

PHILIPPIANS 2:12-13

NIV - *Therefore, my dear friends, as you have always obeyed—not only in my presence, but now much more in my absence—continue to work out your salvation with fear and trembling, for it is God who works in you to will and to act in order to fulfill his good purpose.*

RSV - *Therefore, my beloved, as you have always obeyed, so now, not only as in my presence but much more in my absence, work out your own salvation with fear and trembling; for God is at work in you, both to will and to work for his good pleasure.*

KJV - *Wherefore, my beloved, as ye have always obeyed, not as in my presence only, but now much more in my absence, work out your own salvation with fear and trembling.*
For it is God which worketh in you both to will and to do of his good pleasure.

LB - *Dearest friends, when I was there with you, you were always so careful to follow my instructions. And now that I am away you must be even more careful to do the good things that result from being saved, obeying God with deep reverence, shrinking back from all that might displease him. For God is at work within you, helping you want to obey him, and then helping you do what he wants.*

NOTE TO THE EDUCATOR

We obey because of what He has done for us. He paid it all. He came to serve. Let us work out our own salvation with fear and trembling in the knowledge of His death, resurrection, ascension and return. He is alive and working in us to accomplish all His pleasure. Is this day a pleasure? If it is, to God be the glory for He is at work within you to bring pleasure to those you interact with each day. If your day is not a pleasure, lean into Him for the knowledge, strength and confidence to obey Him and let Him work through you. What are the two great things He wants from us: to love Him and to love others. We can do all things through Him.

1:16 PM PRAYER

Please pray that teachers are encouraged, not discouraged through the evaluation process.

QUOTE FOR THE DAY

If we want a love message to be heard, it has to be sent out. To keep a lamp burning, we have to keep putting oil in it. **Mother Teresa**

NOTES:
_____
_____
_____
_____
_____

DAY 154

#iamachristianeducator

 Where we read the Bible with our brother and sisters in the public schools

DAILY PROMISES OF GOD
for educators

PHILIPPIANS 4:13

NIV - *I can do all this through him who gives me strength.*

RSV - *I can do all things in him who strengthens me.*

KJV - *I can do all things through Christ which strengtheneth me.*

LB - *for I can do everything God asks me to with the help of Christ who gives me the strength and power.*

NOTE TO THE EDUCATOR

You probably have this verse on a wall in your home or calendar somewhere. It's one of the most well-know scriptures and no wonder. We can't do this profession on our own. We can't possibly mold and impact the next generation without Him. We can't serve our colleagues with love without Him. Frankly, we can't do anything with integrity without Him. I have seen this verse on the walls of many offices in public schools. Are you allowed to post it? If it is for your personal encouragement and in your personal space, by all means, yes. Be discreet, be sensitive and represent Him well in all that you do for He is the One Who strengthens you.

1:16 PM PRAYER

Please pray that we prepare our hearts for the celebration of His Resurrection.

QUOTE FOR THE DAY

The great end of life is not knowledge but action. **Thomas H. Huxley**

NOTES:

_____
_____
_____
_____
_____

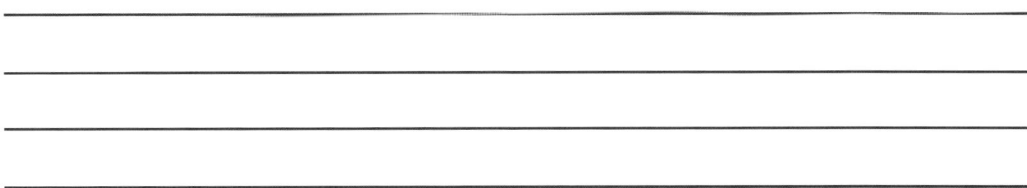
Where we read the Bible with our brother and sisters in the public schools

DAILY PROMISES OF GOD
for educators

PHILIPPIANS 4:19-20

NIV - *And my God will meet all your needs according to the riches of his glory in Christ Jesus. To our God and Father be glory for ever and ever. Amen.*

RSV - *And my God will supply every need of yours according to his riches in glory in Christ Jesus. To our God and Father be glory for ever and ever. Amen.*

KJV - *But my God shall supply all your need according to his riches in glory by Christ Jesus. Now unto God and our Father be glory for ever and ever. Amen.*

LB - *And it is he who will supply all your needs from his riches in glory because of what Christ Jesus has done for us. Now unto God our Father be glory forever and ever. Amen.*

NOTE TO THE EDUCATOR

Needs vs. wants are a struggle for all of us. What do we actually need in our school environments? What do we want? A need may be for safety for our students. A need may be for our lesson planning to be done with integrity that our instruction may provide student engagement. A need may be for our heart to be turned to God that we may teach like Jesus. The good news is that when we pray for our needs, we can say Philippians 4:19-20 with confidence because our God will supply all our needs because He is the Great Educator. May God richly bless you and your students with all your needs.

1:16 PM PRAYER

Please pray to remember that God's promises are on His timing, not ours.

QUOTE FOR THE DAY

You can't build a reputation on what you're going to do. **Henry Ford**

NOTES:
_____
_____
_____
_____
_____

DAY 156

#iamachristianeducator

Where we read the Bible with our brother and sisters in the public schools

DAILY PROMISES OF GOD
for educators

COLOSSIANS 2:13-14

NIV - *When you were dead in your sins and in the uncircumcision of your flesh, God made you alive with Christ. He forgave us all our sins, having canceled the charge of our legal indebtedness, which stood against us and condemned us; he has taken it away, nailing it to the cross.*

RSV - *And you, who were dead in trespasses and the uncircumcision of your flesh, God made alive together with him, having forgiven us all our trespasses, having canceled the bond which stood against us with its legal demands; this he set aside, nailing it to the cross.*

KJV - *And you, being dead in your sins and the uncircumcision of your flesh, hath he quickened together with him, having forgiven you all trespasses; Blotting out the handwriting of ordinances that was against us, which was contrary to us, and took it out of the way, nailing it to his cross;*

LB - *You were dead in sins, and your sinful desires were not yet cut away. Then he gave you a share in the very life of Christ, for he forgave all your sins, and blotted out the charges proved against you, the list of his commandments which you had not obeyed. He took this list of sins and destroyed it by nailing it to Christ's cross.*

NOTE TO THE EDUCATOR

Forgiveness at school is so necessary. Students are being disciplined daily. Teachers are being evaluated constantly. Relationships are strained on a daily basis. A healthy classroom is one where the slate is wiped clean each day. Speaking to our students about forgiveness and then modeling it privately with students who have broken the rules is an outpouring of grace that has been bestowed upon us as Christians. We are called to be peacemakers and whenever it is possible, we need to be the first ones to forgive. After all, look what He did for us.

1:16 PM PRAYER

Please pray that the students are safe on their way home today.

QUOTE FOR THE DAY

Lord, grant that I may always desire more than I accomplish. **Michelangelo**

NOTES:

_____

_____

_____

_____

_____

DAY 157

#iamachristianeducator

 *Where we read the Bible with our brother and sisters in the public schools*

DAILY PROMISES OF GOD
for educators

COLOSSIANS 3:2-3

NIV - *Set your minds on things above, not on earthly things. For you died, and your life is now hidden with Christ in God.*

RSV - *Set your minds on things that are above, not on things that are on earth. For you have died, and your life is hid with Christ in God.*

KJV - *Set your affection on things above, not on things on the earth. For ye are dead, and your life is hid with Christ in God.*

LB - *Let heaven fill your thoughts; don't spend your time worrying about things down here. You should have as little desire for this world as a dead person does. Your real life is in heaven with Christ and God.*

NOTE TO THE EDUCATOR

What does it mean to be an ambassador? You live in a foreign society with laws and even a language that is different than yours. You are sent to represent your home country so that others will see it in a good light. As ambassadors for Christ in the public schools, we live in a culture that has a worldview often different than ours. We are unable to speak the language of our God freely and most importantly we have been sent to represent our future home in a good light that others may be attracted to it. His promises always lead us to His eternal promise to be with Him forever. Bless you Christian ambassador so that you may bless all those you serve each day in our public schools.

1:16 PM PRAYER

Please pray that we may look into the eyes of each of our students with a smile.

QUOTE FOR THE DAY

Act as if what you do makes a difference. It does. **William James**

NOTES:
_____
_____
_____
_____
_____

 Where we read the Bible with our brother and sisters in the public schools

DAILY PROMISES OF GOD
for educators

COLOSSIANS 3:23-24

NIV - *Whatever you do, work at it with all your heart, as working for the Lord, not for human masters, since you know that you will receive an inheritance from the Lord as a reward. It is the Lord Christ you are serving.*

RSV - *Whatever your task, work heartily, as serving the Lord and not men, knowing that from the Lord you will receive the inheritance as your reward; you are serving the Lord Christ.*

KJV - *And whatsoever ye do, do it heartily, as to the Lord, and not unto men; Knowing that of the Lord ye shall receive the reward of the inheritance: for ye serve the Lord Christ.*

LB - *Whatever work you do, do it with all your heart. Do it for the Lord and not for men. Remember that you will get your reward from the Lord. He will give you what you should receive. You are working for the Lord Christ.*

NOTE TO THE EDUCATOR

This is the crux of our high calling. We go into education because the Lord has called us and we know that whatever we do, we are doing it with all our might for Him, not for our supervisors. For example, when we plan a lesson, we do for the Lord, not to be handed in for some checklist. Lesson plans that are done for the Lord will always be better than our own plans because He directs our steps. When it is time to be evaluated, picture Him in the back of your room instead of your administrator. When it's time to go home after an exhausting day, love on your family as you are doing it for the Lord. His reward is so much better than "highly effective" or mastery. His reward is the inheritance!

1:16 PM PRAYER

Please pray to find the teachable moments during the testing season.

QUOTE FOR THE DAY

Take a method and try it. If it fails, admit it frankly, and try another. But by all means, try something. **F. D. Roosevelt**

NOTES:

_____

_____

_____

_____

_____

 Where we read the Bible with our brother and sisters in the public schools

DAILY PROMISES OF GOD
for educators

1ST THESSALONIANS 5:23-24

DAY 160

NIV - *May God himself, the God of peace, sanctify you through and through. May your whole spirit, soul and body be kept blameless at the coming of our Lord Jesus Christ. The one who calls you is faithful, and he will do it.*

RSV - *May the God of peace himself sanctify you wholly; and may your spirit and soul and body be kept sound and blameless at the coming of our Lord Jesus Christ. He who calls you is faithful, and he will do it.*

KJV - *And the very God of peace sanctify you wholly; and I pray God your whole spirit and soul and body be preserved blameless unto the coming of our Lord Jesus Christ.*

LB - *May the God of peace himself make you entirely pure and devoted to God; and may your spirit and soul and body be kept strong and blameless until that day when our Lord Jesus Christ comes back again. God, who called you to become his child, will do all this for you, just as he promised.*

NOTE TO THE EDUCATOR

I love how the Living Bible translates this portion of the verse: *God, who called you to become his child, will do all this for you, just as He promised.* What will He do? He will keep your soul, spirit and body blameless until the coming of the Lord Jesus! What is our part? We need to take care of ourselves mentally, physically and spiritually if we are going to be useful to Him and our students. Are you getting enough rest at night? Make it a non-negotiable. Are you in the Word and prayer each day? Make it a non-negotiable. Are you exercising? Don't laugh. It can be as simple as walking each day. Why not combine it with prayer walking? Christian friend, none of us are good at taking care of all aspects for our lives, but we owe to Him who designed us and to our students who depend on us.

1:16 PM PRAYER

Please pray for the needs of our bus drivers.

QUOTE FOR THE DAY

Knowing is not enough, we must apply. Willing is not enough, we must do. **Goethe**

NOTES:
_____
_____
_____
_____
_____

#iamachristianeducator

 Where we read the Bible with our brother and sisters in the public schools

DAILY PROMISES OF GOD
for educators

2ND THESSALONIANS 3:3

DAY 161

NIV - *But the Lord is faithful, and he will strengthen you and protect you from the evil one.*

RSV - *But the Lord is faithful; he will strengthen you and guard you from evil.*

KJV - *But the Lord is faithful, who shall stablish you, and keep you from evil.*

LB - *But the Lord is faithful; he will make you strong and guard you from satanic attacks of every kind.*

NOTE TO THE EDUCATOR

It is not common to speak about Satan the Devil in our times, however, that doesn't make him any less real. He is the prince and the power of the air. He loves evil and hates those who love the Lord. Our hope lies in the Lord Who has already defeated him. Reject negative or strange thoughts in the name of Jesus. Disregard fiery darts of doubt to discourage you. Know your enemy, but don't play with your enemy. Pray for your students who listen to music that takes them far away from God. Ask the Lord to intervene on their behalf and show them more wholesome ways to spend time under those ear buds.

1:16 PM PRAYER

Please pray to continually be salt and light in our school communities.

QUOTE FOR THE DAY

There is only one way to bring up a child in the way he should go and that is to travel that way yourself. **Abraham Lincoln**

NOTES:

_____

_____

_____

_____

_____

Where we read the Bible with our brother and sisters in the public schools

#iamachristianeducator

DAILY PROMISES OF GOD
for educators

2ND TIMOTHY 2:11-13

NIV - *Here is a trustworthy saying: If we died with him, we will also live with him; if we endure, we will also reign with him. If we disown him, he will also disown us; if we are faithless, he remains faithful, for he cannot disown himself.*

RSV - *The saying is sure: If we have died with him, we shall also live with him; if we endure, we shall also reign with him; if we deny him, he also will deny us; if we are faithless, he remains faithful—for he cannot deny himself.*

KJV - *It is a faithful saying: For if we be dead with him, we shall also live with him: If we suffer, we shall also reign with him: if we deny him, he also will deny us: If we believe not, yet he abideth faithful: he cannot deny himself.*

LB - *I am comforted by this truth, that when we suffer and die for Christ it only means that we will begin living with him in heaven. And if we think that our present service for him is hard, just remember that some day we are going to sit with him and rule with him. But if we give up when we suffer, and turn against Christ, then he must turn against us. Even when we are too weak to have any faith left, he remains faithful to us and will help us, for he cannot disown us who are part of himself, and he will always carry out his promises to us.*

NOTE TO THE EDUCATOR

Our faithful Lord is with you always. He will be faithful even and especially when we are weak for He cannot disown His own. This is security. This is hope. This is His promise throughout the Word. We are a blessed people raised up to bless others. Who have you blessed today? A blessing can be an outreach of any type. It can be a sweet smile to a colleague who is burdened. It can be a hand-written note sent home "just because." Blessings are beautiful. We bless others because He has blessed us first.

1:16 PM PRAYER

Please pray for the needs of our school counselors.

QUOTE FOR THE DAY

Reflect upon your present blessings - of which every man has many - not on your past misfortunes, of which all men have some. **Charles Dickens**

NOTES:
_____
_____
_____
_____
_____

DAY 162

#iamachristianeducator

 Where we read the Bible with our brother and sisters in the public schools

DAILY PROMISES OF GOD
for educators

2ND TIMOTHY 4:8

NIV - *Now there is in store for me the crown of righteousness, which the Lord, the righteous Judge, will award to me on that day—and not only to me, but also to all who have longed for his appearing.*

RSV - *Henceforth there is laid up for me the crown of righteousness, which the Lord, the righteous judge, will award to me on that Day, and not only to me but also to all who have loved his appearing.*

KJV - *Henceforth there is laid up for me a crown of righteousness, which the Lord, the righteous judge, shall give me at that day: and not to me only, but unto all them also that love his appearing.*

LB - *In heaven a crown is waiting for me, which the Lord, the righteous Judge, will give me on that great day of his return. And not just to me but to all those whose lives show that they are eagerly looking forward to his coming back again.*

NOTE TO THE EDUCATOR

Are you looking forward to His return? Do you live for the Day when we will <u>all</u> see Him and stand before Him? Christ followers in every nation eagerly anticipate His coming. The most exciting part for us as Christian educators is our hope that all the students we have ever taught will someday become one of His followers. May our influence through our every day Christ-like actions help them to see Jesus so they will one day long for His coming as well.

1:16 PM PRAYER

Please pray that we reflect His grace in all we say and do today.

QUOTE FOR THE DAY

The object of love is to serve, not to win. **Woodrow Wilson**

NOTES:

_____
_____
_____
_____
_____

DAY 163

#iamachristianeducator

Where we read the Bible with our brother and sisters in the public schools

DAILY PROMISES OF GOD
for educators

TITUS 1:1-3

NIV - *Paul, a servant of God and an apostle of Jesus Christ to further the faith of God's elect and their knowledge of the truth that leads to godliness— in the hope of eternal life, which God, who does not lie, promised before the beginning of time, and which now at his appointed season he has brought to light through the preaching entrusted to me by the command of God our Savior.*

RSV - *Paul, a servant of God and an apostle of Jesus Christ, to further the faith of God's elect and their knowledge of the truth which accords with godliness, in hope of eternal life which God, who never lies, promised ages ago and at the proper time manifested in his word through the preaching with which I have been entrusted by command of God our Savior.*

KJV - *Paul, a servant of God, and an apostle of Jesus Christ, according to the faith of God's elect, and the acknowledging of the truth which is after godliness; In hope of eternal life, which God, that cannot lie, promised before the world began; But hath in due times manifested his word through preaching, which is committed unto me according to the commandment of God our Saviour.*

LB - *Paul, the slave of God and the messenger of Jesus Christ. I have been sent to bring faith to those God has chosen and to teach them to know God's truth—the kind of truth that changes lives—so that they can have eternal life, which God promised them before the world began—and he cannot lie. And now in his own good time he has revealed this Good News and permits me to tell it to everyone. By command of God our Savior, I have been trusted to do this work for him.*

NOTE TO THE EDUCATOR

He is God and He cannot lie. His promise of eternal life is the Good News for all people. Can you imagine what it was like to be Paul and given the ministry of proclaiming the Word to all who will listen? Although you may want to tell everyone the Good News in school, you are a servant of the state and have restrictions. However, there is no law against teaching like Jesus, walking like Jesus, talking like Jesus, inspiring like Jesus. Christian educator, be purposeful in your lifestyle at school and home that He may be glorified.

1:16 PM PRAYER

Please pray for joy for the downtrodden.

QUOTE FOR THE DAY

I have just three things to teach: simplicity, patience, compassion. These three are your greatest treasures. **Lao Tzu**

NOTES:
_____
_____
_____
_____

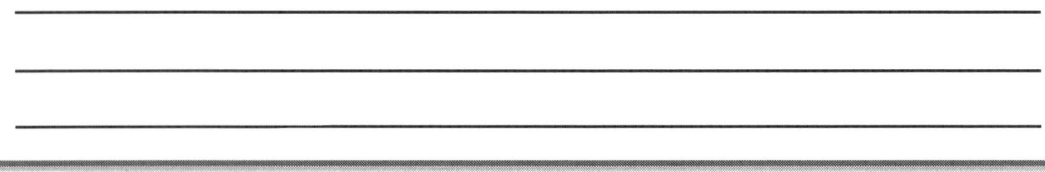

Where we read the Bible with our brother and sisters in the public schools

DAILY PROMISES OF GOD
for educators

HEBREWS 4:9-10

NIV - *There remains, then, a Sabbath-rest for the people of God; for anyone who enters God's rest also rests from their works, just as God did from his.*

RSV - *So then, there remains a sabbath rest for the people of God; for whoever enters God's rest also ceases from his labors as God did from his.*

KJV - *There remaineth therefore a rest to the people of God. For he that is entered into his rest, he also hath ceased from his own works, as God did from his.*

LB - *So there is a full complete rest still waiting for the people of God. Christ has already entered there. He is resting from his work, just as God did after the creation.*

NOTE TO THE EDUCATOR

Rest. Do you get enough rest dear Christian educator? Rest is built into our well-being and when we ignore it, there is no telling how it comes back to bite us. This Sabbath-rest that is our future promise is also God's principle for us today. For the sake of your health and for the good of your students and your family, begin to regulate your sleep and downtimes. Take a whole day and remove yourself from electronics and to-do lists and spend it with God. It sounds so impossible, but it is oh so delightful. Setting aside one day makes the other six days so much more productive. To your mental, physical and spiritual health! Rest.

1:16 PM PRAYER

Please pray that we build each other up and not tear each other down.

QUOTE FOR THE DAY

A prudent question is one half of wisdom. **Francis Bacon**

NOTES:

_____

_____

_____

_____

DAY 165

#iamachristianeducator

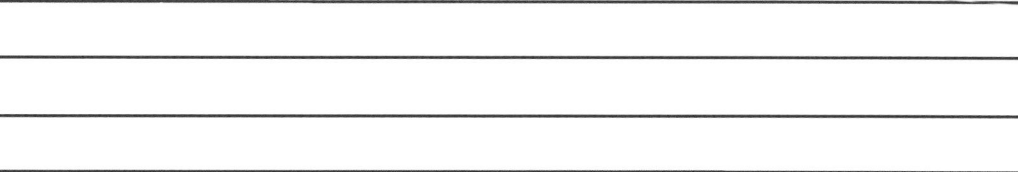

Where we read the Bible with our brother and sisters in the public schools

DAILY PROMISES OF GOD
for educators

HEBREWS 6:10

NIV - *God is not unjust; he will not forget your work and the love you have shown him as you have helped his people and continue to help them.*

RSV - *For God is not so unjust as to overlook your work and the love which you showed for his sake in serving the saints, as you still do.*

KJV - *For God is not unrighteous to forget your work and labour of love, which ye have shewed toward his name, in that ye have ministered to the saints, and do minister.*

LB - *For God is not unfair. How can he forget your hard work for him, or forget the way you used to show your love for him—and still do—by helping his children?*

NOTE TO THE EDUCATOR

The difference between being an educator with a high calling and an educator with a job is the reminder of this promise. Everything we do as Christian educators is for Him. When we help a student in need, we help Him. When we encourage a colleague who is suffering, we help Him. He is ever mindful of our situation and is never unfair or unjust. Pray today for the opportunity to serve someone (student or colleague) who would never expect it. You will be serving Him.

1:16 PM PRAYER

Please pray to recognize that we are image bearers of God.

QUOTE FOR THE DAY

There is within every soul a thirst for happiness and meaning. **Thomas Aquinas**

NOTES:

_____

_____

_____

_____

DAY 166

#iamachristianeducator

Where we read the Bible with our brother and sisters in the public schools

DAILY PROMISES OF GOD
for educators

HEBREWS 6:17

NIV - *Because God wanted to make the unchanging nature of his purpose very clear to the heirs of what was promised, he confirmed it with an oath.*

RSV - *So when God desired to show more convincingly to the heirs of the promise the unchangeable character of his purpose, he interposed with an oath,*

KJV - *Wherein God, willing more abundantly to shew unto the heirs of promise the immutability of his counsel, confirmed it by an oath:*

LB - *God also bound himself with an oath, so that those he promised to help would be perfectly sure and never need to wonder whether he might change his plans.*

NOTE TO THE EDUCATOR

Isn't it comforting to know that God does not change His mind? He has promised eternal life to His heirs and nothing can change that. It is immutable, unchangeable and bound by an oath from Him! Christian educator, we are heirs to His promise. Let us live each day in awe of His eternal gift. Let us praise Him while we are on our way to school, during the day with each need, at 1:16PM in prayer each day with your brothers and sisters in the public schools and on our way home. He is our Promise Keeping Lord.

1:16 PM PRAYER

Please pray for God's protection from false accusations of wrongdoing.

QUOTE FOR THE DAY

Watch your thoughts; they become words.
Watch your words; they become actions.
Watch your actions; they become habits.
Watch your habits; they become character.
Watch your character; for it becomes your destiny. **Author Unknown**

NOTES:

_____
_____
_____
_____

Where we read the Bible with our brother and sisters in the public schools

DAY 167

#iamachristianeducator

DAILY PROMISES OF GOD
for educators

HEBREWS 8:10-12

DAY 168

NIV - *This is the covenant I will establish with the people of Israel after that time, declares the Lord. I will put my laws in their minds and write them on their hearts. I will be their God, and they will be my people. No longer will they teach their neighbor, or say to one another, 'Know the Lord,' because they will all know me, from the least of them to the greatest. For I will forgive their wickedness and will remember their sins no more.*

RSV - *This is the covenant that I will make with the house of Israel after those days, says the Lord: I will put my laws into their minds, and write them on their hearts, and I will be their God, and they shall be my people. And they shall not teach every one his fellow or every one his brother, saying, 'Know the Lord,' for all shall know me, from the least of them to the greatest. For I will be merciful toward their iniquities, and I will remember their sins no more."*

KJV - *For this is the covenant that I will make with the house of Israel after those days, saith the Lord; I will put my laws into their mind, and write them in their hearts: and I will be to them a God, and they shall be to me a people: And they shall not teach every man his neighbour, and every man his brother, saying, Know the Lord: for all shall know me, from the least to the greatest. For I will be merciful to their unrighteousness, and their sins and their iniquities will I remember no more.*

LB - *But this is the new agreement I will make with the people of Israel, says the Lord: I will write my laws in their minds so that they will know what I want them to do without my even telling them, and these laws will be in their hearts so that they will want to obey them, and I will be their God and they shall be my people. And no one then will need to speak to his friend or neighbor or brother, saying, 'You, too, should know the Lord,' because everyone, great and small, will know me already. And I will be merciful to them in their wrongdoings, and I will remember their sins no more.*

NOTE TO THE EDUCATOR

Our gracious, merciful Savior will write His laws on the hearts of everyone in the kingdom. We won't struggle with sin as we do now and we will know in our hearts the right thing to do always. What a beautiful hope we have as we interact with so many that do not know Him YET. In those days, we won't even have to tell them about Him or walk like Him because ALL will know Him and all will desire to be like Him. In the meantime, let us strive to be like Him each and every day at school and when we falter, be encouraged by this high and future hope.

1:16 PM PRAYER

Please pray for endurance for each remaining school day.

QUOTE FOR THE DAY

We turn not older with years, but newer every day. **Emily Dickinson**

NOTES:
_____
_____
_____

#iamachristianeducator

 Where we read the Bible with our brother and sisters in the public schools

DAILY PROMISES OF GOD
for educators

HEBREWS 10:10

NIV - *And by that will, we have been made holy through the sacrifice of the body of Jesus Christ once for all.*

RSV - *And by that will we have been sanctified through the offering of the body of Jesus Christ once for all.*

KJV - *By the which will we are sanctified through the offering of the body of Jesus Christ once for all.*

LB - *Under this new plan we have been forgiven and made clean by Christ's dying for us once and for all.*

NOTE TO THE EDUCATOR

Wouldn't it be amazing to have a classroom where forgiveness could be given once for all? That's obviously the classroom of the kingdom, but praise God for His incredible gift of forgiveness once for all through Jesus Christ our Lord. Probably the best we can do for our students as His servants is to model forgiveness. So many of our students have not experienced true forgiveness. Many will say, "I'm sorry," when they get caught and not really mean it, but what if we could model forgiveness when we make mistakes? Students are always watching us and a heartfelt, compassionate forgiving may wash away a great deal of unnecessary guilt our students bear.

1:16 PM PRAYER

Please pray for those who are grieving the loss of loved ones.

QUOTE FOR THE DAY

Change your thoughts and you change your world. **Norman Vincent Peale**

NOTES:

_____
_____
_____
_____

DAY 169

#iamachristianeducator

 Where we read the Bible with our brother and sisters in the public schools

DAILY PROMISES OF GOD
for educators

HEBREWS 10:23

NIV - *Let us hold unswervingly to the hope we profess, for he who promised is faithful.*

RSV - *Let us hold fast the confession of our hope without wavering, for he who promised is faithful.*

KJV - *Let us hold fast the profession of our faith without wavering; for he is faithful that promised.*

LB - *Now we can look forward to the salvation God has promised us. There is no longer any room for doubt, and we can tell others that salvation is ours, for there is no question that he will do what he says.*

NOTE TO THE EDUCATOR

Our God is faithful. His eternal promise is secured and we can hold on without wavering. What does faithfulness look like in the classroom? Faithfulness often comes in the small things. Do you start your day in prayer for your students? Do you dress professionally? If you teach secondary, your students evaluate your attire daily. It sends a great message of professionalism when you take the time to dress up for them. Do you ask God to give you wisdom? He is willing. Are you compliant to your district curriculum and standards? Do your administrators view you as someone they can rely on? As a Christian educator, your expectations are higher since you work for the Lord first and then your district. Being faithful is not always easy, but it is always rewarding.

1:16 PM PRAYER

Please pray to have a burning desire to change our school community for the better.

QUOTE FOR THE DAY

Well done is better than well said. **Benjamin Franklin**

NOTES:

_____

_____

_____

_____

DAY 170

#iamachristianeducator

Where we read the Bible with our brother and sisters in the public schools

DAILY PROMISES OF GOD
for educators

HEBREWS 10:36

DAY 171

NIV - *You need to persevere so that when you have done the will of God, you will receive what he has promised.*

RSV - *For you have need of endurance, so that you may do the will of God and receive what is promised.*

KJV - *For ye have need of patience, that, after ye have done the will of God, ye might receive the promise.*

LB - *You need to keep on patiently doing God's will if you want him to do for you all that he has promised.*

NOTE TO THE EDUCATOR

What a perfect promise verse for the end of the school year! As we draw near there is a heightened sense of perseverance. What seems like a never-ending school year, suddenly we are finished! I imagine that the kingdom will have a similar feeling. We wait a lifetime to see Jesus and then when we are finally with Him, the wait will be inconsequential. Be very careful to finish strong, my Christian educator. When the tendency is to slow down or plan parties, keep the students working. They will have plenty of time on summer vacation to play. As the old adage goes, "Idle children are the devil's workshop." Let's keep them learning until the end.

1:16 PM PRAYER

Please pray to truly believe that we can do all things through Christ Who is in us.

QUOTE FOR THE DAY

Never be afraid to trust an unknown future to a known God. **Corrie Ten Boom**

NOTES:

_____

_____

_____

_____

#iamachristianeducator

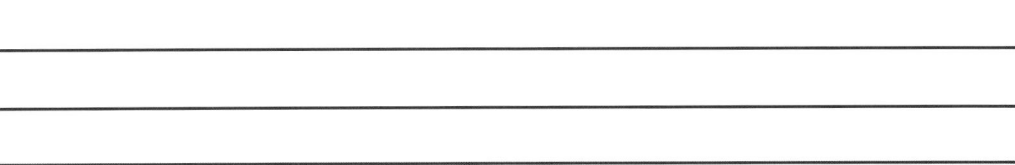
Where we read the Bible with our brother and sisters in the public schools

DAILY PROMISES OF GOD
for educators

HEBREWS 11:6

DAY 172

NIV - *And without faith it is impossible to please God, because anyone who comes to him must believe that he exists and that he rewards those who earnestly seek him.*

RSV - *And without faith it is impossible to please him. For whoever would draw near to God must believe that he exists and that he rewards those who seek him.*

KJV - *But without faith it is impossible to please him: for he that cometh to God must believe that he is, and that he is a rewarder of them that diligently seek him.*

LB - *You can never please God without faith, without depending on him. Anyone who wants to come to God must believe that there is a God and that he rewards those who sincerely look for him.*

NOTE TO THE EDUCATOR

God's promises are true whether we believe them or not. This promise in Hebrews 11:6 spells out the conditions:
- We must have faith in Him.
- We please Him when we believe that He exists.
- We believe that He rewards those who seek Him.
- We are dependent upon Him for all our needs.

As Christian educators we stand firm in our faith that God has purposed us to be His servants in the public schools and that He will give us all we need to serve our students and colleagues. Hallelujah to our King!

1:16 PM PRAYER

Please pray for impact through the National Day of Prayer.

QUOTE FOR THE DAY

Even if I knew that tomorrow the world would go to pieces, I would still plant my apple tree.
Martin Luther

NOTES:
_____
_____
_____
_____

#iamachristianeducator

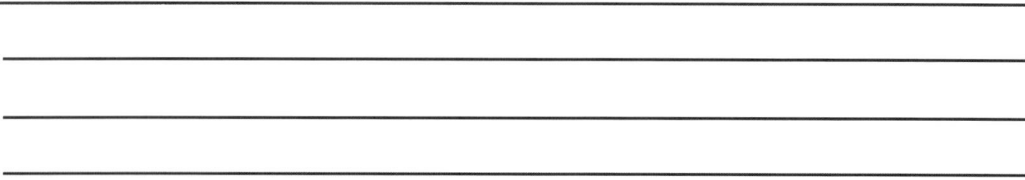
Where we read the Bible with our brother and sisters in the public schools

DAILY PROMISES OF GOD
for educators

HEBREWS 13:5

DAY 173

NIV - *Keep your lives free from the love of money and be content with what you have, because God has said, Never will I leave you; never will I forsake you.*

RSV - *Keep your life free from love of money, and be content with what you have; for he has said, I will never fail you nor forsake you.*

KJV - *Let your conversation be without covetousness; and be content with such things as ye have: for he hath said, I will never leave thee, nor forsake thee.*

LB - *Stay away from the love of money; be satisfied with what you have. For God has said, I will never, never fail you nor forsake you.*

NOTE TO THE EDUCATOR

I don't think anyone will ever accuse us of going into education for the love of money! The second part of the verse states that we are to be content with what we have. Contentment is not only with our salary, but our schedules, our teammates, our students, our administrators and our parents. Being a good steward of our income is critical since it doesn't change a whole lot each year. My husband and I struggled with debt most of our adult years on a teacher's salary, but once we understood this promise we took the Dave Ramsey Financial Peace Class. We broke through and are totally debt free now! It can be done. Contentment is a whole lot easier when you have no debt. Even though the last part of the verse doesn't seem that it goes with the first part, He will never leave you or forsake through all issues. We now have only the debt to love. No matter what your salary is, if you have debt, please take a Biblically based course to help you become debt free.

1:16 PM PRAYER

Please pray that a spirit of cooperation is a priority.

QUOTE FOR THE DAY

By the choices and acts of our lives, we create the person that we are. **Kenneth Patton (adapted)**

NOTES:
___
___
___
___

#iamachristianeducator

 Where we read the Bible with our brother and sisters in the public schools

DAILY PROMISES OF GOD
for educators

HEBREWS 13:20-21

NIV - *Now may the God of peace, who through the blood of the eternal covenant brought back from the dead our Lord Jesus, that great Shepherd of the sheep, equip you with everything good for doing his will, and may he work in us what is pleasing to him, through Jesus Christ, to whom be glory for ever and ever. Amen.*

RSV - *Now may the God of peace who brought again from the dead our Lord Jesus, the great shepherd of the sheep, by the blood of the eternal covenant, equip you with everything good that you may do his will, working in you that which is pleasing in his sight, through Jesus Christ; to whom be glory for ever and ever. Amen.*

KJV - *Now the God of peace, that brought again from the dead our Lord Jesus, that great shepherd of the sheep, through the blood of the everlasting covenant, Make you perfect in every good work to do his will, working in you that which is wellpleasing in his sight, through Jesus Christ; to whom be glory for ever and ever. Amen.*

LB - *And now may the God of peace, who brought again from the dead our Lord Jesus, equip you with all you need for doing his will. May he who became the great Shepherd of the sheep by an everlasting agreement between God and you, signed with his blood, produce in you through the power of Christ all that is pleasing to him. To him be glory forever and ever. Amen.*

NOTE TO THE EDUCATOR

As we enter the school house door, we walk with the Great Shepherd of the sheep Who signed the everlasting covenant with His blood. What can possibly defeat us? What can remove us from His will for us? When pressures rise in the lunchroom, the teachers' lounge, the hallways, cafeteria, offices and classrooms read these verses. He is the God of Peace. He is the Covenant Keeping Lord and He will work in us to do what is pleasing in His sight. May the God of Peace bless you and your students in these final days of the year. May He shine His Face on you and your students and may He turn His countenance towards you and give you peace. Amen.

1:16 PM PRAYER

Please pray for the students and colleagues who are going through divorce.

QUOTE FOR THE DAY

Every accomplishment starts with the decision to try. **Gail Devers**

NOTES:

_____
_____
_____
_____

DAY 174

#iamachristianeducator

 *Where we read the Bible with our brother and sisters in the public schools*

DAILY PROMISES OF GOD
for educators

JAMES 1:5

DAY 175

NIV - *If any of you lacks wisdom, you should ask God, who gives generously to all without finding fault, and it will be given to you.*

RSV - *If any of you lacks wisdom, let him ask God, who gives to all men generously and without reproaching, and it will be given him.*

KJV - *If any of you lack wisdom, let him ask of God, that giveth to all men liberally, and upbraideth not; and it shall be given him.*

LB - *If you want to know what God wants you to do, ask him, and he will gladly tell you, for he is always ready to give a bountiful supply of wisdom to all who ask him; he will not resent it.*

NOTE TO THE EDUCATOR

You have not because you ask not. Can you believe this promise? God is ready, willing and able to bestow wisdom on us if we ask. He won't even think we are foolish. Asking for wisdom as an educator may be the smartest thing we can ever do. We may know our content, but do we have the wisdom to teach the lesson in a manner that our students can learn? Ask God to help you. It's a guarantee that He will give you what you need. If you lack the wisdom to handle difficult discipline problems this year, ask God because He has promised to give you wisdom liberally. As the school year comes to a close, thoughts and dreams of next year are always on our minds. Don't make any decisions or plans without asking for His wisdom first. He knows what we need and what is best for us. He's just waiting for you to ask.

1:16 PM PRAYER

Please pray for protection for teachers and students while driving to school.

QUOTE FOR THE DAY

The strongest principle of growth lies in the human choice. **George Eliot**

NOTES:

_____

_____

_____

_____

#iamachristianeducator

  Where we read the Bible with our brother and sisters in the public schools

DAILY PROMISES OF GOD
for educators

JAMES 2:5

NIV - *Listen, my dear brothers and sisters: Has not God chosen those who are poor in the eyes of the world to be rich in faith and to inherit the kingdom he promised those who love him?*

RSV - *Listen, my beloved brethren. Has not God chosen those who are poor in the world to be rich in faith and heirs of the kingdom which he has promised to those who love him?*

KJV - *Hearken, my beloved brethren, Hath not God chosen the poor of this world rich in faith, and heirs of the kingdom which he hath promised to them that love him?*

LB - *Listen to me, dear brothers: God has chosen poor people to be rich in faith, and the Kingdom of Heaven is theirs, for that is the gift God has promised to all those who love him.*

NOTE TO THE EDUCATOR

This is what we love about our Lord. He didn't choose us because we are famous and brilliant. He didn't choose us because we are better than others. He chooses the weak of the world, those who are poor in the eyes of the famous to be rich in faith towards Him.

Dear Lord,
   Thank you Lord for Your promise of the inheritance to us. We do not deserve it and we are in awe that we can enter into the kingdom because of what You have done. You are love. We long to be in community with You and humbly adore Your presence in our schools. Thank You Lord for choosing us to represent You. Help us Lord to get out of the way and let You lead. Bless this day, O King. We love You.
Amen.

1:16 PM PRAYER

Please pray that we remember that we have a Father Who loves us and is crazy about us.

QUOTE FOR THE DAY

Our lives were meant for calm, not chaos. **Thomas Kinkade**

NOTES:
_____
_____
_____
_____

DAY 176

#iamachristianeducator

Where we read the Bible with our brother and sisters in the public schools

DAILY PROMISES OF GOD
for educators

JAMES 4:8

D A Y 1 7 7

NIV - *Come near to God and he will come near to you. Wash your hands, you sinners, and purify your hearts, you double-minded.*

RSV - *Draw near to God and he will draw near to you. Cleanse your hands, you sinners, and purify your hearts, you men of double mind.*

KJV - *Draw nigh to God, and he will draw nigh to you. Cleanse your hands, ye sinners; and purify your hearts, ye double minded.*

LB - *And when you draw close to God, God will draw close to you. Wash your hands, you sinners, and let your hearts be filled with God alone to make them pure and true to him.*

NOTE TO THE EDUCATOR

Don't you just want to shout it on the mountains. Don't you want to go out and tell all the world. Draw close to God and He will draw close to you! It's a promise! In our role as educator we can't just shout it on the mountains, nor tell it to all the people in our official capacity as a government employee, but we can pray this promise over our students and colleagues. We can walk our daily lives like we believe this truth. We can sing praises to God in our hearts throughout the day and be blessed by the Word of God during our quiet times at school. (if you can find any!) When we take one step toward God, it is as if He takes two steps towards us. Please take time this summer to draw close to God and see what He has in store for you.

1:16 PM PRAYER

Please pray for opportunities to serve on committees and boards where our influence would make a difference for Christ and the Truth.

QUOTE FOR THE DAY

Finish each day before you begin the next, and interpose a solid wall of sleep between the two.
Ralph Waldo Emerson

NOTES:

_____

_____

_____

_____

#iamachristianeducator

Where we read the Bible with our brother and sisters in the public schools

DAILY PROMISES OF GOD
for educators

JAMES 5:14-15

NIV - *Is anyone among you sick? Let them call the elders of the church to pray over them and anoint them with oil in the name of the Lord. And the prayer offered in faith will make the sick person well; the Lord will raise them up. If they have sinned, they will be forgiven.*

RSV - *Is any among you sick? Let him call for the elders of the church, and let them pray over him, anointing him with oil in the name of the Lord; and the prayer of faith will save the sick man, and the Lord will raise him up; and if he has committed sins, he will be forgiven.*

KJV - *Is any sick among you? let him call for the elders of the church; and let them pray over him, anointing him with oil in the name of the Lord: And the prayer of faith shall save the sick, and the Lord shall raise him up; and if he have committed sins, they shall be forgiven him.*

LB - *Is anyone sick? He should call for the elders of the church and they should pray over him and pour a little oil upon him, calling on the Lord to heal him. And their prayer, if offered in faith, will heal him, for the Lord will make him well; and if his sickness was caused by some sin, the Lord will forgive him.*

NOTE TO THE EDUCATOR

Is there any sickness on your campus? On any given day, someone is sick among us. The degree of the sickness may vary, but one of our most important ministries of service as Christian educators is to pray for the sick among us. We are also charged to call the elders of our church to come and pray over them and anoint them with oil. Bring this idea to your church and ask if you can call upon the elders to come to your school next year for those who are extremely ill. How sweet would it be for a local church to adopt your school and know that the elders are willing and able to come to pray and anoint when needed? Please pray about this principle of Christian living and bring it to your prayer group for agreement.

1:16 PM PRAYER

Please pray for the Body of Christ to surround our schools in prayer.

QUOTE FOR THE DAY

A well-spent day brings happy sleep. **Leonardo daVinci**

NOTES:

_____

_____

_____

_____

DAY 178

#iamachristianeducator

Where we read the Bible with our brother and sisters in the public schools

DAILY PROMISES OF GOD
for educators

1ST PETER 1:24-25

NIV - *All people are like grass, and all their glory is like the flowers of the field; the grass withers and the flowers fall, but the word of the Lord endures forever. And this is the word that was preached to you.*

RSV – *All flesh is like grass and all its glory like the flower of grass. The grass withers, and the flower falls, but the word of the Lord abides for ever. That word is the good news which was preached to you.*

KJV - *For all flesh is as grass, and all the glory of man as the flower of grass. The grass withereth, and the flower thereof falleth away: But the word of the Lord endureth for ever. And this is the word which by the gospel is preached unto you.*

LB - *Yes, our natural lives will fade as grass does when it becomes all brown and dry. All our greatness is like a flower that droops and falls; but the Word of the Lord will last forever. And his message is the Good News that was preached to you.*

NOTE TO THE EDUCATOR

We have studied the promises of God this school year because we invest in the Word of God that will endure forever. As we look back on this school year, we can see the wisdom of the Word reminding us of our temporary existence. This school year is about to fade like the flowers of the grass. Our students will move onto other grades and other teachers. Our positions and curriculum will most likely change, but the one constant in our lives is the Word of God. It stands as the lamp unto our feet and the light unto our path. Be in the Word this summer, my dear Christian educator, to gain wisdom and acknowledge His way.

1:16 PM PRAYER

Please pray for safety at upcoming graduation ceremonies and wisdom for the graduates.

QUOTE FOR THE DAY

Life is like a ten-speed bicycle. Most of us have gears we never use. **Charles Schultz**

NOTES:
_____
_____
_____
_____

Where we read the Bible with our brother and sisters in the public schools

DAILY PROMISES OF GOD
for educators

1ST PETER 3:9

DAY 180

NIV - *Do not repay evil with evil or insult with insult. On the contrary, repay evil with blessing, because to this you were called so that you may inherit a blessing.*

RSV – *Do not return evil for evil or reviling for reviling; but on the contrary bless, for to this you have been called, that you may obtain a blessing.*

KJV - *Not rendering evil for evil, or railing for railing: but contrariwise blessing; knowing that ye are thereunto called, that ye should inherit a blessing.*

LB - *Don't repay evil for evil. Don't snap back at those who say unkind things about you. Instead, pray for God's help for them, for we are to be kind to others, and God will bless us for it.*

NOTE TO THE EDUCATOR

We are to be kind to others and God will bless us for it. Let's pray for a spirit of blessing on our campuses. Our public schools can be one of the meanest places. Students hurt other students' feelings; colleagues can be harmful to each other. As Christians on campus, we need to show a better way – the way of blessing. When someone hurts us, we pray for them first, forgive them next and then bless them. If we consistently and intentionally bless our enemies, it will stand as an unforgettable model. Some may count it as weakness, but we count it as the way of our Lord.

1:16 PM PRAYER

Please pray that God will give our graduates a double blessing of wisdom.

QUOTE FOR THE DAY

Any concern too small to be turned into a prayer is too small to be made into a burden.
Corrie Ten Boom

NOTES:
_____
_____
_____
_____

#iamachristianeducator

 Where we read the Bible with our brother and sisters in the public schools

DAILY PROMISES OF GOD
for educators

1ST PETER 4:14

DAY 181

NIV - *If you are insulted because of the name of Christ, you are blessed, for the Spirit of glory and of God rests on you.*

RSV - *If you are reproached for the name of Christ, you are blessed, because the spirit of glory and of God rests upon you.*

KJV - *If ye be reproached for the name of Christ, happy are ye; for the spirit of glory and of God resteth upon you: on their part he is evil spoken of, but on your part he is glorified.*

LB - *Be happy if you are cursed and insulted for being a Christian, for when that happens the Spirit of God will come upon you with great glory.*

NOTE TO THE EDUCATOR

I don't know about you, but one of my greatest fears is that I will deny Christ when it is a life and death situation. Intellectually, I will stand for Christ no matter what. Emotionally, I pray that I am not weak. This promise is an anchor for us as we walk our walk as Christians in the public schools. There is no power higher than our powerful God. If we are insulted because of what we believe in Him, count it all joy. There have been many sermons that ask, "*If you were in a court of law for being a Christian, would there be enough evidence to convict you?*" May it be so that we can have the glory of God rest on us.

1:16 PM PRAYER

Please pray for the needs of our principals.

QUOTE FOR THE DAY

True friends are those who really know you but love you anyway. **Edna Buchanan**

NOTES:
_____
_____
_____
_____

Where we read the Bible with our brother and sisters in the public schools

DAILY PROMISES OF GOD
for educators

1ST PETER 5:4

DAY 182

NIV - *And when the Chief Shepherd appears, you will receive the crown of glory that will never fade away.*

RSV - *And when the chief Shepherd is manifested you will obtain the unfading crown of glory.*

KJV - *And when the chief Shepherd shall appear, ye shall receive a crown of glory that fadeth not away.*

LB - *And when the Head Shepherd comes, your reward will be a never-ending share in his glory and honor.*

NOTE TO THE EDUCATOR

The Brooklyn Tabernacle Choir sings a great song, "*Soon and Very Soon.*" I can hear them in my mind saying, "Soon and very soon, we are going to see the King. Soon and very soon, we are going to see the King. Soon and very soon, we are going to see the King. Hallelujah, Hallelujah, we are going to see the King." This is what we are waiting for. This is what helps us through the school day. This is the call on our life to motivate us, to encourage us and to equip to remain steadfast, immovable and ever-abounding in the work of the Lord. Never forget dear brother and sister, that your labor in the Lord is never in vain.

1:16 PM PRAYER

Please pray to remember that Jesus is our peace.

QUOTE FOR THE DAY

Things turn out best for the people who make the best of the way things turn out. **John Wooden**

NOTES:
_____
_____
_____
_____

#iamachristianeducator

 Where we read the Bible with our brother and sisters in the public schools

DAILY PROMISES OF GOD
for educators

1ST PETER 5:6-7

DAY 183

NIV - *Humble yourselves, therefore, under God's mighty hand, that he may lift you up in due time. Cast all your anxiety on him because he cares for you.*

RSV - *Humble yourselves therefore under the mighty hand of God, that in due time he may exalt you. Cast all your anxieties on him, for he cares about you.*

KJV - *Humble yourselves therefore under the mighty hand of God, that he may exalt you in due time: Casting all your care upon him; for he careth for you.*

LB - *If you will humble yourselves under the mighty hand of God, in his good time he will lift you up. Let him have all your worries and cares, for he is always thinking about you and watching everything that concerns you.*

NOTE TO THE EDUCATOR

The natural inclination when we begin to pray is to bow our heads in humility. When we are humble, we are in a position to hear our dear Lord. When we feel overwhelmed in school, the remedy is to humble ourselves. When we are troubled, we need to take our anxieties and literally cast them upon Him. He loves us so much that He wants to remove the burdens from us, but we have to cast them upon Him believing that He is a Promise Keeper Who will lift us up in due time. Be patient. He will help.

1:16 PM PRAYER

Please pray for those who have interviews for new positions for next school year.

QUOTE FOR THE DAY

Come to me, all you who are weary and burdened, and I will give you rest. **Jesus Christ**

NOTES:
_____
_____
_____
_____

#iamachristianeducator

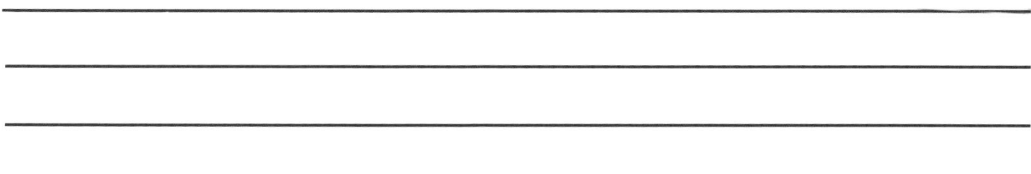
Where we read the Bible with our brother and sisters in the public schools

DAILY PROMISES OF GOD
for educators

2ND PETER 1:4

NIV - *Through these he has given us his very great and precious promises, so that through them you may participate in the divine nature, having escaped the corruption in the world caused by evil desires.*

RSV - *By which he has granted to us his precious and very great promises, that through these you may escape from the corruption that is in the world because of passion, and become partakers of the divine nature.*

KJV - *Whereby are given unto us exceeding great and precious promises: that by these ye might be partakers of the divine nature, having escaped the corruption that is in the world through lust.*

LB - *And by that same mighty power he has given us all the other rich and wonderful blessings he promised; for instance, the promise to save us from the lust and rottenness all around us, and to give us his own character.*

NOTE TO THE EDUCATOR

We talk a lot about being "Jesus with skin on" in the public schools since we have restrictions placed on how and what we can say from the front of the classroom. We strive to be like Jesus and show Jesus in our actions and words, but if we are doing it all on our own power, we are doomed to frustration. Our Lord has promised that you can participate in His divine nature through Him and need not try to forge our own way. Let us pray for all Christian educators in the public school to be partakers of the divine nature.

1:16 PM PRAYER

Please pray to be like Joseph knowing that God's plans and promises will be carried out.

QUOTE FOR THE DAY

If you want to live a long life, focus on making contributions. **Hans Selye**

NOTES:

_____
_____
_____
_____

DAY 184

#iamachristianeducator

 Where we read the Bible with our brother and sisters in the public schools

DAILY PROMISES OF GOD
for educators

2ND PETER 2:9

NIV - *If this is so, then the Lord knows how to rescue the godly from trials and to hold the unrighteous for punishment on the day of judgment.*

RSV - *Then the Lord knows how to rescue the godly from trial, and to keep the unrighteous under punishment until the day of judgment.*

KJV - *The Lord knoweth how to deliver the godly out of temptations, and to reserve the unjust unto the day of judgment to be punished.*

LB - *So also the Lord can rescue you and me from the temptations that surround us, and continue to punish the ungodly until the day of final judgment comes.*

NOTE TO THE EDUCATOR

Dear Lord,

We have so many lost students and colleagues in our public schools who do not have the privilege and life changing gift of Jesus in their lives – yet! Lord, we stand in the gap for our students that they may know You and live a life devoted to You. Lord, we lift up our colleagues who are suffering because of sins of commission and sins of omission. Lord, call them. Help them to listen and learn and come into the Body of Christ. For who knows if You have not placed us with them for such a time as this? Amen.

1:16 PM PRAYER

Please pray to remember those who died in wars that we may be free.

QUOTE FOR THE DAY

You can't help getting older, but you don't have to get old. **George Burns**

NOTES:

_____

_____

_____

_____

DAY 1885

#iamachristianeducator

Where we read the Bible with our brother and sisters in the public schools

DAILY PROMISES OF GOD
for educators

2ND PETER 3:13

NIV - *But in keeping with his promise we are looking forward to a new heaven and a new earth, where righteousness dwells.*

RSV - *But according to his promise we wait for new heavens and a new earth in which righteousness dwells.*

KJV - *Nevertheless we, according to his promise, look for new heavens and a new earth, wherein dwelleth righteousness.*

LB - *But we are looking forward to God's promise of new heavens and a new earth afterwards, where there will be only goodness.*

NOTE TO THE EDUCATOR

Hallelujah, Praise God! The Ultimate Promise we all await is the coming of the new heavens and new earth. It's just as Mercy Me sings, "I Can Only Imagine" when they describe what it might be like to finally meet Jesus. You are so close to the end of the year. You may have even finished. It's time to reflect and look to spiritual matters. Our school lives are all-consuming but they never take precedence over our heavenly aspirations. No matter what kind of year this has been, can we give thanks to God for His favor, protection and care? Can we spend more time with Him this summer preparing for next year? Hallelujah, Praise God!

1:16 PM PRAYER

Please pray to finish strong.

QUOTE FOR THE DAY

Promise me you'll remember, you are braver than you believe, stronger than you seem, smarter than you think." **A. A. Milne, Winnie the Pooh**

NOTES:
_____
_____
_____
_____

DAY 1886

#iamachristianeducator

 Where we read the Bible with our brother and sisters in the public schools

DAILY PROMISES OF GOD
for educators

1ST JOHN 1:7

DAY 187

NIV - *But if we walk in the light, as he is in the light, we have fellowship with one another, and the blood of Jesus, his Son, purifies us from all sin.*

RSV - *But if we walk in the light, as he is in the light, we have fellowship with one another, and the blood of Jesus his Son cleanses us from all sin.*

KJV - *But if we walk in the light, as he is in the light, we have fellowship one with another, and the blood of Jesus Christ his Son cleanseth us from all sin.*

LB - *But if we are living in the light of God's presence, just as Christ does, then we have wonderful fellowship and joy with each other, and the blood of Jesus his Son cleanses us from every sin.*

NOTE TO THE EDUCATOR

This promise is a call to gather. Are you praying with other Christians on your campus? Are you planning works of service that represent Him well? Are you writing cards to those who are downtrodden? Walking in the light means being like Jesus. It's a most unique path. There has never been nor will ever be anyone like Him, yet He has given us His Holy Spirit that dwells within us to help us be more like Him each day. Pray for others who will come alongside you to bless your campus particularly for the upcoming school year.

1:16 PM PRAYER

Please pray Prov. 22:6 - Train a child in the way he should go and when he is old he will not turn from it.

QUOTE FOR THE DAY

A person's a person, no matter how small. **Dr. Seuss**

NOTES:
_____
_____
_____
_____

#iamachristianeducator

Where we read the Bible with our brother and sisters in the public schools

DAILY PROMISES OF GOD
for educators

1ST JOHN 1:9

DAY 188

NIV - *If we confess our sins, he is faithful and just and will forgive us our sins and purify us from all unrighteousness.*

RSV - *If we confess our sins, he is faithful and just, and will forgive our sins and cleanse us from all unrighteousness.*

KJV - *If we confess our sins, he is faithful and just to forgive us our sins, and to cleanse us from all unrighteousness.*

LB - *But if we confess our sins to him, he can be depended on to forgive us and to cleanse us from every wrong. And it is perfectly proper for God to do this for us because Christ died to wash away our sins.*

NOTE TO THE EDUCATOR

Why is it so hard to confess? Is it because it's embarrassing or because we can just ignore it and maybe it will go away? 1st John 1:9 is one of the greatest promises God has given us that takes an action on our part in order for Him to do His part. *If* we confess our sins, it's a guarantee that He will forgive them. In fact, He already has. There's something so powerful about confessing as He then cleanses us from all unrighteousness. What are the mistakes and sins you would like to have opportunity to do over next school year? Take them and confess to your Lord and you will truly start with a clean slate new year.

1:16 PM PRAYER

Please pray for genuine attention given to lessons taught today.

QUOTE FOR THE DAY

No act of kindness, no matter how small, is ever wasted. **Aesop**

NOTES:
_____
_____
_____
_____

#iamachristianeducator

Where we read the Bible with our brother and sisters in the public schools

DAILY PROMISES OF GOD
for educators

1ST JOHN 2:17

NIV - *The world and its desires pass away, but whoever does the will of God lives forever.*

RSV - *And the world passes away, and the lust of it; but he who does the will of God abides for ever.*

KJV - *And the world passeth away, and the lust thereof: but he that doeth the will of God abideth for ever.*

LB - *And this world is fading away, and these evil, forbidden things will go with it, but whoever keeps doing the will of God will live forever.*

NOTE TO THE EDUCATOR

Have you asked God for His will for you? Have you asked Him what He has purposed you to do? Sometimes He just likes you to ask. One thing is for sure. If you have been doing the Daily Promises of God to this point, you are a Christian educator who has a high calling as His servant in the public schools. That's huge! You may be the only Jesus your children meet. You may be the only one who loves unconditionally. I encourage you to ask God all summer about His plans for you. His ways are higher than our ways and His thoughts are higher than our thoughts. You may be in for a delightful surprise. You have not because you ask not!

1:16 PM PRAYER

Please pray to be a positive example during times of drama at the end of the year.

QUOTE FOR THE DAY

There's no place like home. **L. Frank Braum, The Wizard of Oz**

NOTES:

_____

_____

_____

_____

DAY 189

#iamachristianeducator

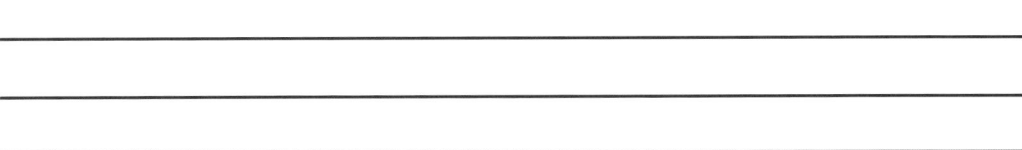
Where we read the Bible with our brother and sisters in the public schools

DAILY PROMISES OF GOD
for educators

1ST JOHN 2:27

DAY 190

NIV - *As for you, the anointing you received from him remains in you, and you do not need anyone to teach you. But as his anointing teaches you about all things and as that anointing is real, not counterfeit—just as it has taught you, remain in him.*

RSV - *But the anointing which you received from him abides in you, and you have no need that any one should teach you; as his anointing teaches you about everything, and is true, and is no lie, just as it has taught you, abide in him.*

KJV - *But the anointing which ye have received of him abideth in you, and ye need not that any man teach you: but as the same anointing teacheth you of all things, and is truth, and is no lie, and even as it hath taught you, ye shall abide in him.*

LB - *But you have received the Holy Spirit, and he lives within you, in your hearts, so that you don't need anyone to teach you what is right. For he teaches you all things, and he is the Truth, and no liar; and so, just as he has said, you must live in Christ, never to depart from him.*

NOTE TO THE EDUCATOR

Abide in Him for He lives in you. The anointing of the Holy Spirit is powerful and He is the Overcomer of all things. What does this have to do with our days in school? Everything! When problems arise, the Holy Spirit will guide you to make the right decision. Listen. When troubles comes for others, you are an intercessor on their behalf whether it is for a child or an adult. When great things happen, the Holy Spirit in you rejoices with you and with those who rejoice. He will never leave you, it's a sealed deal. Rise up Christian educators. You are a great gift to our public schools through the guidance of your anointing.

1:16 PM PRAYER

Please pray for protection for the students from any evil plans of others.

QUOTE FOR THE DAY

Piglet: *"How do you spell love?"* **Pooh:** *"You don't spell it, you feel it."*

NOTES:

_____

_____

_____

_____

#iamachristianeducator

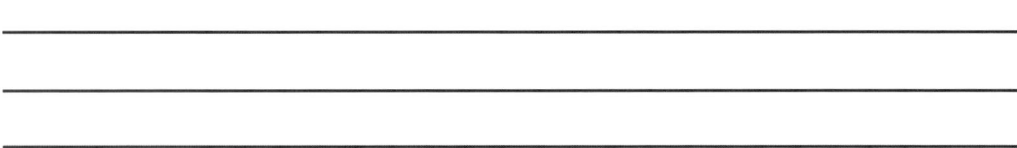
Where we read the Bible with our brother and sisters in the public schools

DAILY PROMISES OF GOD
for educators

1ST JOHN 3:2

NIV - *Dear friends, now we are children of God, and what we will be has not yet been made known. But we know that when Christ appears, we shall be like him, for we shall see him as he is.*

RSV - *Beloved, we are God's children now; it does not yet appear what we shall be, but we know that when he appears we shall be like him, for we shall see him as he is.*

KJV - *Beloved, now are we the sons of God, and it doth not yet appear what we shall be: but we know that, when he shall appear, we shall be like him; for we shall see him as he is.*

LB - *Yes, dear friends, we are already God's children, right now, and we can't even imagine what it is going to be like later on. But we do know this, that when he comes we will be like him, as a result of seeing him as he really is.*

NOTE TO THE EDUCATOR

Dear Lord,
   Thank You for making us Your children. It is with great anticipation that we long to see You at Your coming. Help us Lord, to live lives rich in the Fruit of the Holy Spirit. Help us to lean on You for everything because in the end, we will be like You! During this journey, help us to grow in our relationships with our colleagues and with our students. Teach us to number our days that we treasure them all to Your glory. We love you and proclaim this joy in the unmatched Name of Jesus Christ. Amen.

1:16 PM PRAYER

Please pray that all students and educators be guarded in body, mind and spirit this summer vacation.

QUOTE FOR THE DAY

In every job that must be done, there is an element of fun. You find the fun, and the job's a game.
P.L. Travers, Mary Poppins

NOTES:
_____
_____
_____
_____

DAY 191

#iamachristianeducator

Where we read the Bible with our brother and sisters in the public schools

DAILY PROMISES OF GOD
for educators

1ST JOHN 4:16-17

NIV - *And so we know and rely on the love God has for us. God is love. Whoever lives in love lives in God, and God in them. This is how love is made complete among us so that we will have confidence on the day of judgment: In this world we are like Jesus.*

RSV - *So we know and believe the love God has for us. God is love, and he who abides in love abides in God, and God abides in him. In this is love perfected with us, that we may have confidence for the day of judgment, because as he is so are we in this world.*

KJV - *And we have known and believed the love that God hath to us. God is love; and he that dwelleth in love dwelleth in God, and God in him. Herein is our love made perfect, that we may have boldness in the day of judgment: because as he is, so are we in this world.*

LB - *We know how much God loves us because we have felt his love and because we believe him when he tells us that he loves us dearly. God is love, and anyone who lives in love is living with God and God is living in him. And as we live with Christ, our love grows more perfect and complete; so we will not be ashamed and embarrassed at the day of judgment, but can face him with confidence and joy because he loves us and we love him too.*

NOTE TO THE EDUCATOR

God loves us so dearly. We love Him because He first loved us. In this promise of abiding, we have confidence in the present and future to stand boldly in His love. Let us set our hearts on the next school year to make a commitment to love our students and colleagues in a way we never had. Let our prayers over the summer be for God to show us how to love like He does. Let's practice on our families this summer and come back to school for a year of love. What does that look like? It means seeing each child and colleague through His eyes. It means praying for them regularly. It means taking the first step in reconciliation. Ask Him what it should look like at your school. He will show you ways you have never imagined because He loves you.

1:16 PM PRAYER

Please pray to encourage our students to serve.

QUOTE FOR THE DAY

Never judge someone by the way he looks or a book by the way it's covered; for inside those tattered pages, there's a lot to be discovered. **Stephen Cosgrove, Serendipity**

NOTES:

_____

_____

_____

_____

DAY 192

#iamachristianeducator

 Where we read the Bible with our brother and sisters in the public schools

DAILY PROMISES OF GOD
for educators

1ST JOHN 5:14

DAY 1993

NIV - *This is the confidence we have in approaching God: that if we ask anything according to his will, he hears us.*

RSV - *And this is the confidence which we have in him, that if we ask anything according to his will he hears us.*

KJV - *And this is the confidence that we have in him, that, if we ask any thing according to his will, he heareth us.*

LB - *And we are sure of this, that he will listen to us whenever we ask him for anything in line with his will.*

NOTE TO THE EDUCATOR

How do you know you are in line with His will? How do you know you are praying for something that is according to His plan for us? The answer is in the Manual, our Handbook, the Word of God. When you read the Bible over and over it is amazing how it has the answer to every one of life's dilemmas. It is living and active, sharper than any two-edged sword, piercing to the division of soul and spirit, of joints and marrow, and discerning the thoughts and intentions of the heart. (Hebrews 4:12) There is no other book like the Bible. In fact, I've heard it said, *"I have read many books in my life, but the Bible is the only book that reads me."* Go confidently before the Lord with your petitions when you ask according to His Word.

1:16 PM PRAYER

Please pray to extend goodness to our colleagues and students.

QUOTE FOR THE DAY

"What day is it?" asked Pooh. "It's today," squeaked Piglet. "My favorite day," said Pooh
A.A. Milne, Winnie the Pooh

NOTES:
_____
_____
_____
_____

#iamachristianeducator

 Where we read the Bible with our brother and sisters in the public schools

DAILY PROMISES OF GOD
for educators

1ST JOHN 5:18

NIV - *We know that anyone born of God does not continue to sin; the One who was born of God keeps them safe, and the evil one cannot harm them..*

RSV - *We know that any one born of God does not sin, but He who was born of God keeps him, and the evil one does not touch him.*

KJV - *We know that whosoever is born of God sinneth not; but he that is begotten of God keepeth himself, and that wicked one toucheth him not.*

LB - *No one who has become part of God's family makes a practice of sinning, for Christ, God's Son, holds him securely, and the devil cannot get his hands on him.*

NOTE TO THE EDUCATOR

I know that I continue to sin. It is not my intention, but I fall. Yet I am secure in Him, the One Who shed His blood for us for the forgiveness of sin once for all. That is unbelievable. How can we have such a Great Savior? By His mercy and grace we are saved and freed to sin no more. When you sin, and you will, cast your heart upon His throne and sin no more. Don't give the devil an opportunity to put ideas of worthlessness or hopelessness in your mind. Those thoughts are never from God. Allow only thoughts of love, joy and peace to invade your mindset and ask for His help when you fall. What a precious sacrifice He has made for us, for our students, for our colleagues and for all who believe. Bless His Holy Name, Jesus.

1:16 PM PRAYER

We must all face the choice between what is right and what is easy.
J.K. Rowling, Harry Potter and the Goblet of Fire

QUOTE FOR THE DAY

We must all face the choice between what is right and what is easy.
J.K. Rowling, Harry Potter and the Goblet of Fire

NOTES:

_____
_____
_____
_____

DAY 194

#iamachristianeducator

 Where we read the Bible with our brother and sisters in the public schools

DAILY PROMISES OF GOD
for educators

REVELATION 2:7

NIV - *Whoever has ears, let them hear what the Spirit says to the churches. To the one who is victorious, I will give the right to eat from the tree of life, which is in the paradise of God.*

RSV - *He who has an ear, let him hear what the Spirit says to the churches. To him who conquers I will grant to eat of the tree of life, which is in the paradise of God.*

KJV - *He that hath an ear, let him hear what the Spirit saith unto the churches; To him that overcometh will I give to eat of the tree of life, which is in the midst of the paradise of God.*

LB - *Let this message sink into the ears of anyone who listens to what the Spirit is saying to the churches: To everyone who is victorious, I will give fruit from the Tree of Life in the Paradise of God.*

NOTE TO THE EDUCATOR

Well done good and faithful servant, you have been faithful this school year. You are an overcomer if you made it through the whole school year. You are victorious. Perhaps it was your best year ever, praise God. Maybe it was the worst year, praise God for His grace to complete this school year. What if this school year was neither great nor bad? Ask for a sharpening of your toolbox this summer. Ask God to show you any indifference or attitudes you need to change. Be all you can be next school year and persevere because You are called to be His servant and you have this rich reward waiting for you in eternity. What could be more important?

1:16 PM PRAYER

Please pray that we ask God what He wants us to do this summer.

QUOTE FOR THE DAY

What you see and what you hear depends a great deal on where you are standing. **C.S. Lewis**

NOTES:
_____
_____
_____
_____

Where we read the Bible with our brother and sisters in the public schools

DAILY PROMISES OF GOD
for educators

REVELATION 3:5

NIV - *The one who is victorious will, like them, be dressed in white. I will never blot out the name of that person from the book of life, but will acknowledge that name before my Father and his angels.*

RSV - *He who conquers shall be clad thus in white garments, and I will not blot his name out of the book of life; I will confess his name before my Father and before his angels.*

KJV - *He that overcometh, the same shall be clothed in white raiment; and I will not blot out his name out of the book of life, but I will confess his name before my Father, and before his angels.*

LB - *Everyone who conquers will be clothed in white, and I will not erase his name from the Book of Life, but I will announce before my Father and his angels that he is mine.*

NOTE TO THE EDUCATOR

What if we had a day when all Christian educators wore white to school? It would be our symbol of hope in this incredible promise. Let's do it. I am proclaiming the first Wednesday after Labor Day as **"Clothed in White Day"** to unite all Christians in the public schools to proclaim their belief that one day all His saints (us!) will be dressed in white with our names written in the Book of Life while He announces our names before our Father and His angels. What a celebration it will be. Help me spread the word. It may start small, but who knows how far it can reach with the power of the Holy Spirit.

1:16 PM PRAYER

Please pray for God's wisdom and guidance in our high calling.

QUOTE FOR THE DAY

Education is the most powerful weapon which you can use to change the world. **Nelson Mandela**

NOTES:

_____
_____
_____
_____

DAY 1996

#iamachristianeducator

 Where we read the Bible with our brother and sisters in the public schools

DAILY PROMISES OF GOD
for educators

REVELATION 3:12-13

NIV - *The one who is victorious I will make a pillar in the temple of my God. Never again will they leave it. I will write on them the name of my God and the name of the city of my God, the new Jerusalem, which is coming down out of heaven from my God; and I will also write on them my new name. Whoever has ears, let them hear what the Spirit says to the churches..*

RSV - *He who conquers, I will make him a pillar in the temple of my God; never shall he go out of it, and I will write on him the name of my God, and the name of the city of my God, the new Jerusalem which comes down from my God out of heaven, and my own new name. He who has an ear, let him hear what the Spirit says to the churches.*

KJV - *Him that overcometh will I make a pillar in the temple of my God, and he shall go no more out: and I will write upon him the name of my God, and the name of the city of my God, which is new Jerusalem, which cometh down out of heaven from my God: and I will write upon him my new name. He that hath an ear, let him hear what the Spirit saith unto the churches.*

LB - *As for the one who conquers, I will make him a pillar in the temple of my God; he will be secure and will go out no more; and I will write my God's Name on him, and he will be a citizen in the city of my God—the New Jerusalem, coming down from heaven from my God; and he will have my new Name inscribed upon him. Let all who can hear listen to what the Spirit is saying to the churches.*

NOTE TO THE EDUCATOR

I had a friend who taught 6th grade Science and she gave all her students new names. It was so funny because she was able to remember their new names right away, but took several weeks before she knew their real names. Can you imagine what it is going to be like when God writes His Name on us and we will know Jesus's new Name? While we are still in our earthly bodies, we wear the name of Christian, a Christ-follower. Let that name be written on our daily lives that others may come to know Him as we do. Praise God for His amazing plans for us in all eternity.

1:16 PM PRAYER

Please pray to be in God's Word this summer.

QUOTE FOR THE DAY

The function of education is to teach one to think intensively and to think critically. Intelligence plus character - that is the goal of true education. **Martin Luther King, Jr.**

NOTES:

___

DAY 197

#iamachristianeducator

 *Where we read the Bible with our brother and sisters in the public schools*

DAILY PROMISES OF GOD
for educators

REVELATION 3:21

NIV - *To the one who is victorious, I will give the right to sit with me on my throne, just as I was victorious and sat down with my Father on his throne.*

RSV - *He who conquers, I will grant him to sit with me on my throne, as I myself conquered and sat down with my Father on his throne.*

KJV - *To him that overcometh will I grant to sit with me in my throne, even as I also overcame, and am set down with my Father in his throne.*

LB - *I will let everyone who conquers sit beside me on my throne, just as I took my place with my Father on his throne when I had conquered.*

NOTE TO THE EDUCATOR

Christian educators are conquerors. Walking our faith in the public schools and ministering to our students and teachers under the law is a tightrope walk. Learning your boundaries is essential to being an effective witness. If you have not already done so, join our movement of Christian educators across the country who understand the value of unity by going to www.ceai.org. We send you encouragement, legal information and tips for living out your faith. As you fulfill your ministry to your students and possibly your colleagues, you will never know how many people will be called as a result of your faithfulness. You are a conqueror because you have overcome the obstacles of walking your walk. May God continue to bless you with opportunities to grow anew each and every school year.

1:16 PM PRAYER

Please pray for the summer plans of the students and staff.

QUOTE FOR THE DAY

The whole purpose of education is to turn mirrors into windows. **Sydney J. Harris**

NOTES:

_____
_____
_____
_____

 Where we read the Bible with our brother and sisters in the public schools

DAILY PROMISES OF GOD
for educators

REVELATION 21:4

NIV - *He will wipe every tear from their eyes. There will be no more death or mourning or crying or pain, for the old order of things has passed away.*

RSV - *He will wipe away every tear from their eyes, and death shall be no more, neither shall there be mourning nor crying nor pain any more, for the former things have passed away.*

KJV - *And God shall wipe away all tears from their eyes; and there shall be no more death, neither sorrow, nor crying, neither shall there be any more pain: for the former things are passed away.*

LB - *He will wipe away all tears from their eyes, and there shall be no more death, nor sorrow, nor crying, nor pain. All of that has gone forever.*

NOTE TO THE EDUCATOR

We anxiously await a time when there will be no more tears, no more pain and no more death. I can't wait to see what it will be like when sin is not crouching at our door. "Thy kingdom come" in the Lord's prayer is my favorite part because it focuses all His promises in one concise statement. We can't wait. We live in earthly bodies in a sin sick world with no hope if we don't know God's promises. So many of our students have no idea they are living in temporary bodies in a temporary time, but one day we will rejoice when they see Jesus and call Him Lord and Savior. What a great day that will be!

1:16 PM PRAYER

Please pray to remember the small things today and be faithful so that God can use us for bigger things tomorrow.

QUOTE FOR THE DAY

Education is not the filling of a pail, but the lighting of a fire. **William Butler Yeats**

NOTES:

_____
_____
_____
_____

DAY 199

#iamachristianeducator

Where we read the Bible with our brother and sisters in the public schools

DAILY PROMISES OF GOD
for educators

REVELATION 22:4-5

NIV - *They will see his face, and his name will be on their foreheads. There will be no more night. They will not need the light of a lamp or the light of the sun, for the Lord God will give them light. And they will reign for ever and ever.*

RSV - *They shall see his face, and his name shall be on their foreheads. And night shall be no more; they need no light of lamp or sun, for the Lord God will be their light, and they shall reign for ever and ever.*

KJV - *And they shall see his face; and his name shall be in their foreheads. And there shall be no night there; and they need no candle, neither light of the sun; for the Lord God giveth them light: and they shall reign for ever and ever.*

LB - *And they shall see his face; and his name shall be written on their foreheads. And there will be no night there—no need for lamps or sun—for the Lord God will be their light; and they shall reign forever and ever.*

NOTE TO THE EDUCATOR

Awesome God, our Father,

As we draw to the end of the Daily Promises for Educators and the close of this school year, we rejoice in Your promises. They have been a feast, Lord and have planted us firmly in the ultimate promise of eternal life through the shed blood, death, resurrection and ascension of Your Son Jesus Christ. Thank You for being a Promise Keeping God and loving us into the kingdom. Lord, please bless the children over the summer and return them to us with dreams and visions from You. Thank you Lord for this beautiful journey through Your Word. We love you so much. Amen.

1:16 PM PRAYER

Praise God for this past school year. Have a blessed summer!

QUOTE FOR THE DAY

Give a man a fish and you feed him for a day; teach a man to fish and you feed him for a lifetime.
Maimonides

NOTES:

_____

_____

_____

_____

DAY 200

#iamachristianeducator

Where we read the Bible with our brother and sisters in the public schools

DAILY PROMISES OF GOD
for educators

FINAL THOUGHTS

My dearest Christian educator,

    Thank you for investing in the reading of the Promises of God for Educators this school year. I can't tell you enough how wonderful it is to be joined with our brothers and sisters in the public schools in prayer and in the Word of God. Yours is a high calling. It is one of the gifts of the church to be a teacher along with pastors, evangelists and prophets. (Ephesians 4:11-13) When you go through the schoolhouse door, you are not only an educator paid by the state, but more importantly a teacher ambassador for Christ. It doesn't matter what position you hold: bus driver, crossing guard, teacher, cafeteria worker, custodian, secretary, coach, substitute, administrator or technician, you are a Christian first and and educator second. Once you grasp the significance of your placement at that school for such a time as this, it changes your mindset. Instead of grumbling, you praise. Instead of gossiping, you compliment. Instead of worrying, you cast your cares upon Him who cares. Instead of looking to the district for the latest pedagogy, You look to the Author of everything.

    We are in a unique position in the public schools because we are state employees. In a sense, that makes us "Congress" when you look at the First Amendment. *"Congress shall make no law respecting an establishment of religion, or prohibiting the free exercise thereof; or abridging the freedom of speech, or of the press; or the right of the people peaceably to assemble, and to petition the Government for a redress of grievances."* Simply put – when you are on the "clock" you cannot establish a religion in your classroom or school. No proselytizing. However, our students are not bound by any restrictions except that they may not interrupt instructional time. When you take off your "Congress" hat before or after you are on the "clock" you maintain your 1st Amendment privileges as any other American. As a Christian, we want to always be legal and graceful representatives. Do everything in your power to love. Be wise as a serpent and harmless as a dove.

    I encourage you to use this Companion every school year. Look to the Word for His promises on a daily basis. His Word is living and active and sharper than any two-edged sword. Please share with your colleagues and remind them that they are not alone. We have thousands of brothers and sisters throughout the public schools who believe that God can transform our public schools with His love and truth. It has been an amazing privilege to encourage, equip and empower you with the tools of prayer and His promises. May He show You His purpose for your life through His Word and your prayers.

Prayerfully yours,
Karen C. Seddon

www.ccai.org
www.one16pray.com
www.aw180days.com
http://the16-9movement.blogspot.com
http://get.theapp.co/394c
#iamachristianeducator

www.aw180days.com

#iamachristianeducator

 Where we read the Bible with our brother and sisters in the public schools

Made in the USA
Lexington, KY
27 August 2017